The Grown-Up's Guide to Running Away from Home

The Grown-Up's Guide to Running Away from Home

by

ROSANNE KNORR

Ten Speed Press
Berkeley, California

🔟

Ten Speed Press
P.O. Box 7123
Berkeley, California 94707
www.tenspeed.com

Distributed in Australia by Simon and Schuster Australia, in Canada by Ten Speed Press Canada, in New Zealand by Tandem Press, in South Africa by Real Books, in Southeast Asia by Berkeley Books, and in the United Kingdom and Europe by Airlift Books.

Cover design by Kathy Warinner
Cover illustration by Kathy Warinner
Interior design by Laura Lind Design

Library of Congress Cataloging-in-Publication Data

Knorr, Rosanne.
        The grown-up's guide to running away from home / by Rosanne Knorr.
            p.   cm.
        Includes bibliographical references and index.
        ISBN 1-58008-000-6
        1. Retirement, Places of—Foreign countries. 2. Americans–
    –Foreign countries. 3. Retirees—Life skills guides. I. Title.
        HQ1063.K65   1998   98-8126
        646.7'9—dc21   CIP

First printing 1998
Printed in Canada

1 2 3 4 5 6 7 8 9 10 — 02 01 00 99 98

To John,
for dreaming and sharing
the grown-up adventure

To Jennifer,
for enthusiasm and the card that
wouldn't let Mom "wimp out"

Contents

Acknowledgments

For sharing advice and tales from their adventures, I want to thank the following grown-ups: Frank Anderson, Frances Aronson, Anne Berra, Bob Berra, Rulon Brown, Mary Campbell, Treasa Campbell, Craig Cantor, Sue Chambers, Jim Chambers, Pam deLyra, Steve deLyra, Edward Flaherty, Douglas Gilbert, Joanne Kenady, Karen Kenady, Barbara Kopczyski, Claire Larson, Judy Lawrence, Jim Lowenthal, Dick Mackin, Betts Marriott, Ed Marriott, Margot Milner, Dave Oswald, Susan Oswald, Ben Ott, Maria-Eugenia Ott, Shannon Roxborough, Peter Vaughan, Doug Wallis, Starr Wallis, Getra White, Steve White, and Dana Wood.

For reading, advising, editing, and otherwise aiding this effort, special thanks to John Knorr, Lynne Marriott, Kirsty Melville, Jennifer Piascik, and Aaron Wehner.

Thanks, also, to the shy who didn't want recognition. Other than that, if I've forgotten anyone, please forgive a poor memory.

Note to Readers

Every care has been taken to ensure that this book is accurate and inspiring. I hope it provides you a base from which to explore the countless options available, helping you revitalize your adult years with a long-term adventure overseas.

However, this book is not intended as the end point, but the beginning from which to launch your own adventure. It cannot substitute for the professional assistance of accountants, lawyers, tax experts, travel agents, and other specialists involved in your making a transition overseas. You must investigate and make informed decisions based on your personal and financial situation.

While, to the best of my knowledge, this material is accurate, resources change locations and telephone numbers, services offered, and regulations. As you make specific plans, investigate fully and carefully. Neither I, nor the publishers, can take any responsibility for the outcome of actions you take based on reading this book.

If, in the course of your investigations, you discover additional information or corrections that would be helpful when this book is updated, please contact the author in care of the publisher.

Many thanks and may your adventure overseas provide fulfillment and happiness beyond your dreams.

Introduction

Long, long ago—before career ladders and children and homes with mortgages to be paid on a regular basis—I dreamed of sipping wine at a French café with a view of the Eiffel Tower or waking to the day in a whitewashed cottage on a Greek island. You could fill in your own dreams. We all have them.

But for most of us, the travel through life follows a practical path. As we reach middle age, it's our children, the students in high school or college, who participate in a year abroad. We see them and say, "I wish I could have done that." Then, one day, my husband and I asked, "Why can't we do it now?"

Midlife is an ideal time for adventure overseas. The empty nest provides the opportunity to "run away" from the humdrum habits of several decades and create a fulfilling second life. As my husband commented: "I've done this life. I want to have another."

So here we sit today in our little French village house. We're discovering new tastes in food and wine. We're meeting fascinating people and exploring different cultures. We're learning a new language and studying art, and our French home serves as a European base. We can take off for driving trips to Italy, Spain, Portugal, and beyond—each trip a new adventure in itself. Best of all, we're seeing it all for ourselves, with a freshness and spirit of adventure that's putting new sparkle into these middle years. Now, after spending years raising our kids, we're the kids we wanted to be. You can take that literally.

One wonderful result of our adventure is the realization that gaining knowledge of the world is the true fountain of youth. Like children, we're busy discovering the world again, after all these old years of living. We don't worry or wonder just what it is we'll do with the rest of our years now that kids and work are behind us, as I hear some people our ages complain. No, we're too busy comparing the latest wines with our neighbors, exploring medieval churches and museums, participating fully in town life here, while planning the trips to nearby regions and countries. Our life is full and, as the French say, *agréable*. We're doing what we want when we want, a dream we never thought could become a reality, but which proved to be amazingly easy to accomplish.

You too can achieve this freedom. Enjoy a year, or more, of life overseas. Relish that feeling of discovery. It's *not* just for the young. And, when you return to your old life—if you choose to return—you'll bring new interests and an intriguing mystique home. If you return to work, you'll add an international perspective to your career.

Running away from home as an adult *does* take more planning than it does for a younger person. When we were younger we had nothing to lose if we took off for a year or more. We didn't have jobs, or at least not ones that paid enough to matter at that point. No children or elderly parents to be concerned about. No home with a mortgage, filled with stuff. Any belongings we did have could be stashed at our parents' house until our return.

But we are the parents now. We have the houses packed with the accumulation of a lifetime. The mere thought of arranging a year off is intimidating enough to make anyone want to plop back in front of the TV with an old movie and a beer. In our case, the itch for adventure was still there at ages fifty and sixty-one. We needed to scratch the itch while we were still young enough to negotiate old-world cobblestone streets, or we would forever regret not doing it.

So we searched libraries and bookstores. We made idiots of ourselves asking people if they'd ever lived overseas. Many people answered in the affirmative, and we grilled them on how they had arranged the countless details. Their input helped make this book possible. (Some of their attitudes and comments are reflected in quotes scattered throughout this book.) We discovered a range of attitudes toward living this type of adventure. The brave souls simply up and went. The not-so-brave (or more generously, less foolhardy!), like us, talked it over and over. But they still dreamed.

Most of all, the number of midlifers who had successfully achieved an extended leave encouraged us. I started studying what they did to achieve their dreams. For five years before our departure, I looked for others who had done what we planned. I interviewed them, found out where they went and why, asked how they planned their adventures, and determined what worked and what didn't. We found the areas we were interested in and took our vacations in those places, watching for the resident Americans of San Miguel or Ajijic or Aix-en-Provence. (If a person spoke English but didn't carry a camera, it was a clue they weren't the average tourist!) They proved to be friendly, informative, and most important, inspiring.

Finally, we narrowed down our destination and studied up on the country we wanted as our overseas base—France. We joined Alliance Française, the worldwide group that promotes French culture and language. We practiced our *bonjour*. But were we brave enough to follow our dream?

Gradually, we uncovered the details that would make our adventure overseas possible. We discovered the best means of divesting ourselves of our home and belongings, staying in touch with our family, friends, and financial advisors—and we even planned how to take our only "child" still at home, a pound puppy named Folly. The details we needed weren't found in any book, so we were left to seek out others who had taken the road we wanted to follow, or invent the solutions for ourselves.

We found far more adult adventurers than I had thought possible. The reasons they gave for "escaping" overseas were varied, but boiled down to a few basics: They'd had the long hours at work. They'd had the pressures of conformity. They'd had the so-called "good life" of stateside suburbia. Now they wanted to experience more of the world and a different lifestyle before the rocking chair became their mode of transportation.

Our plans were both frightening and exhilarating. The suburban life we had lived for decades was about to be turned topsy turvy. But that was the point. Escaping must be an adventure, or it's simply more of the same. The true joy of living overseas on a long-term sabbatical or retirement is that you become alive to a host of possibilities that would otherwise be lost in the routine of a life you already know, perhaps too well.

If the thought of new discoveries after forty intrigues you, then I urge you to read on. If you decide on such an adventure, I hope this book helps you, too, to plan, prepare, and gain confidence that such an experience is not only possible, but the experience of a lifetime.

As you hoist your backpack (well, OK, roll-on luggage), just tell the kids who look on enviously that, after all these years, it's your turn for adventure.

1

The Psyche Behind the Escapee

A MAN IS NOT OLD UNTIL
REGRETS TAKE THE PLACE OF DREAMS.
—John Barrymore

Look around you at the people we call middle-aged today. They're playing tennis and jogging. They're eating their oat bran, cutting out smoking, and trying in general to behave themselves so they can look forward to another thirty or more years of life. With better health care and healthier lifestyles, today's adults at forty, fifty, sixty, or more still have a lot to look forward to. Or do they?

They've had a career. Or rather, a career may have had them. Downsizing and buyouts in the early nineties have taken their toll. In fact, the changes of that era hit middle-class midlifers harder than any other age group. Though today's economy is stronger, the older worker (heck, even younger ones) has discovered that the "contract" between employer and employee doesn't exist anymore. Not only that, burned-out workers don't want the contract, because suddenly work is not the be-all and end-all of existence.

The social fabric in the United States is changing in a way that impacts how people, especially us older ones, view work and its relationship to our lives. The era of single-minded devotion to one's job is being eclipsed by a desire for more time: time to spend with family, time to spend on hobbies, time to spend traveling and seeing this big, wonderful world.

It's natural. After years of ceaselessly striving for "success," many adults, most of them baby boomers, are burnt out. They've done it all. Now that they're where they wanted to be—or realizing they won't ever be there—the smart ones are reevaluating their lives and discovering new possibilities.

Lots of life is left to live after the kids are grown and gone. What will you do with those years? More of the same? Will you repeat the same year of experience for another ten or twenty years? Or will you seek out new experiences? The escapee answers with the latter.

> *All too often I have patients who say, "I'm fifty and my life is over." They don't see a future. Having an adventure is a beginning, opening up a whole new chapter of possibilities.*
> —Dr. Laura Robinson, Ph.D., Psychology

Who Escapes Overseas?

- An escapee could be a baby boomer who worked hard and believed the good life was up ahead—but burnout or downsizing got them first.
- Traditional retirees who finally have the time they've always wanted to enjoy a second lifestyle are often expatriates. Their rocking chair is going to have a view of the Mediterranean, thank you.
- An early retiree with a hefty buyout package, who's ready to explore new possibilities for fulfillment is in a great position to make the escape.
- Anyone can be an escapee who's ready for an exhilarating experience that will lift their spirits and give them a reason to feel like a kid again.

> *There's a certain stage in your life when there's something you want to do besides go to work.*
> —Peter, 60, Saint Senoch, France

The Shift in American Values

A *Money* magazine survey in 1994 determined that nearly one in five Americans were thinking about moving abroad, one in four college-educated adults. This interest in long-term travel or overseas living is just part of the shift now occurring throughout the United States. Driven by baby boomers who don't want to settle for a lackluster life, people are choosing time for family, home, and hobbies over climbing the corporate ladder.

In a survey released by Robert Half International, the average worker would exchange a shorter workweek for less pay—a 21 percent pay cut in exchange for 21 percent less time on the job. Women are even more eager than men to gain time. Asked whether they would give up rapid career advancement for more family or personal time, 76 percent of female respondents said yes.

This attitude is driving the exodus overseas. More Americans are discovering that other countries often offer a calmer, more tranquil way of life—or a more exciting one, depending on the destination. Most of all, Americans are beginning to understand that there's more to life than their usual routine, and they're heading out in ever increasing numbers to explore it.

> *America has long been a promised land . . . but an increasing*
> *number of Americans are looking abroad for the chance to live the*
> *kind of life they don't believe is possible in the U.S. I've seen some who*
> *are lookingfor a slower, morepeaceful pace and view a declining*
> *quality of life in the States. Others are seeking economic*
> *opportunities, fame, or adventure.*
>
> —Shannon Roxborough, country contact, American
> Citizens Abroad, Dominican Republic

Overseas Isn't Out of This World

If you're the typical American, you may be surprised just how many people have taken the step overseas for a year or more. Before we did it, we thought that moving overseas, even temporarily, would be a complicated ritual, akin to moving to Mars.

Now, however, we see the numbers of Americans overseas. We just never ran into them at the corner store. No one else does either, which may explain some of the strange questions we were asked when we first talked of trying life overseas.

In fact, the trend toward Americans moving overseas is gaining momentum. A recent front-page article in the *International Herald Tribune* reported that "the number of Americans living abroad has more than quadrupled in the past 30 years as Americans retire in countries where living costs are lower, return to their ancestral homes, or move abroad to do business or pursue other activities."

The U.S. State Department estimates that currently 3.3 million Americans live abroad, up by more than 1 million in the 1990s alone. The actual count is undoubtedly much higher. Even the State Department admits that many Americans who live overseas either full- or part-time are never counted in the statistics. The State Department has no accurate system for keeping track of all Americans overseas, especially those who may be living temporarily abroad or are retired but retain close ties to the States. Their families are in the United States; their Social Security checks are deposited into a bank there; they may have a mailing address there; and some expats even live part-time, switching regularly from the United States to other countries. Unless they contact the embassy or consulate, they're not counted in the statistics.

FOUR SILLY QUESTIONS EVERY EXPAT IS ASKED

Americans who choose to live overseas for longer than the two-week vacation face some strange comments—even from otherwise intelligent people. The first is, perhaps, the silliest: "Don't you lose your citizenship?" Of course, the answer is no. I guess the people who ask this never considered that U.S. diplomats live overseas as part of the job description, as do business and military personnel, students, and countless other loyal Americans who simply want to expand their worldview. Once you have U.S. citizenship, you never lose it unless you renounce it deliberately or commit some heinous treason. Living on Spain's Costa Brava for a year—or even the rest of your life—won't do it.

The second question people overseas hear is "Don't you love your country?" All I can imagine is that some people confuse the word *expatriate*, which means to live outside of your native country, with *ex-patriot*, which, of course, means a former patriot. A long-term adventure or life overseas has nothing to do with patriotism or love of country, but everything to do with expanding your personal borders to enjoy a more vital life.

The third silly question heard is "Are you willing to give up your ties to the U.S.?" Of course not. In fact, many people who live overseas long-term become members of special organizations, such as American Citizens Abroad, which provide a U.S. connection and support.

A fourth question is, of course, related to the above: "You can't vote, can you?" The answer is yes, you can vote. Americans overseas vote just the way anyone traveling can vote: by absentee ballot. Embassies supply them. Americans abroad keep up with the political situation in the States as people in Cincinnati or Seattle do. They read newspapers and magazines and watch television (CNN and NBC are on satellite overseas). They care about their country and its future. After all, they have history there, families there, investments there, and most of them will be back there themselves when the adventure has run its course.

Sorry Tales of Escapees Who Didn't Read This Book

F. Scott Fitzgerald (1896–1940) and Zelda Fitzgerald (1900-1949)
The American writer and his wife left their Long Island home for the French Riviera in 1924. They didn't return to the United States until 1931. Though his writing about the "lost generation" of American expats in France made him famous, he became an alcoholic; she ended up in an insane asylum.

Paul Gauguin (1848–1903)
Gauguin's an example of nonplanned, irresponsible running away. A successful Paris stockbroker, he left his comfortable life to paint in the South Seas. Though he became famous for his expressive color and design, he died a ruined man. His family, including five children, had to return to his wife's parents to survive.

Ernest Hemingway (1899–1961)
The American writer left his job as a reporter to volunteer as an ambulance driver in Italy during World War I. He later settled in Paris. The adventurous Hemingway spent long periods in Spain, Africa, and Cuba. However, we don't recommend you follow in his footsteps; he drank prodigiously and died a suicide.

Don't worry. By reading this book before you escape overseas, you'll plan your adventure much better than any of the above!

Imagination is fine, but you need to create and take chances.
—Frank, 53, Bangkok, Thailand

Traits of the Successful Escape Artist

People often dream of adventure overseas, and many have already discovered that it's not only possible, but a vital new experience they wouldn't have missed, well, not for all the world. Throughout this book, you'll discover what they did right (and what they did wrong) to help you prepare and ensure that your adventure is a success.

Amazingly enough, many modern-day runaways would at first tell you they're "impetuous" or they'd say they did it "on a whim." That may seem the case to them because an adventure tends to feel that way. In speaking to these people at length, however, it's clear that they actually made calculated decisions. Claire and Dick in Portugal, for example, traveled extensively before they bought their property in Portugal. They used it only for vacations, while renting it out the remainder of the year. After five years, they quit their jobs and moved permanently. Meanwhile, they had five years to consider all aspects of the move. Though their families think they're crazy, they've spent more time planning the move than most people do in planning their families.

It does take solid preparation and a modicum of self-confidence to successfully escape. But this is one adventure that doesn't require Indiana Jones–style bravery. Though a step out of the routine can be a bit intimidating, anything can be handled with some preparation. That's why you're reading this book. You can have a long-term adventure overseas, just as hundreds of thousands of people have done before you. The way is prepared, and what at first seems intimidating becomes matter-of-fact once you know the secrets.

Will you revitalize your midlife by trying on a new lifestyle? Or are you content with maintaining the status quo? Only you can decide. I do know that when a friend asked if I was frightened of making such a major change, I quickly responded, "I'm more afraid of later regretting that I *didn't* do it."

2

Are You Prepared to Pack It In?

THE BEAUTIFUL SOULS ARE
THEY THAT ARE UNIVERSAL, OPEN,
AND READY FOR ALL THINGS.
—Michel de Montaigne

Some people are content to stay put. They are born, raised, schooled, married, and buried in the same town. Others have a wanderlust and travel from the time they can crawl. Then there are the midlifers who blend the two. They have stayed put for most of their lives, building careers and raising families, but at midlife they discover an urge to see the world, to experience a broader dimension than what can be seen every day, around the corner, or on a two-week vacation.

We may have only one life, but that doesn't mean it has to be the same throughout. Do you have thirty, forty, or fifty different years of experience in living? Or the same year several times over? If the answer is the latter and you're not satisfied with those repeated experiences, then you may be ready to try your wings.

Most people who plan long-term adventures overseas have one thing in common: the desire to revitalize themselves and experience more variety from life. Over and over, you hear the same refrain from expatriates: "I didn't want to reach the end and realize I hadn't done this," "I didn't want to do the same old thing until I was an old thing," or "I didn't want to look back on my life and say, "If only I could have . . . .""

Don't let fear stop you. An adventure abroad is easier than you think. With a bit of preparation and patience, you can open up a whole new realm of possibilities for the second half of your life. Your decision, of course, should be based on your own needs and current situation. There's a time to run away and a time to stay put. But if you are ready and the time is right, you too can enjoy the experience of a lifetime.

Start by deciding if this is a good time to plan such an adventure. As much as I encourage you to enjoy the adventure, I do believe that a dream doesn't mean you should throw caution aside, tell your boss to shove it, divorce your spouse, and split.

As an adult, especially, you have special needs that a younger person doesn't have. If you have a good job, then you have a lot invested in it (of course, if you were really happy at that job, then you wouldn't be reading this book). Even if you do want to take a sabbatical, you may find it difficult to return to a comparable position. You may be close to retirement and may not want to endanger your nest egg with an ill-conceived or premature attempt at running away.

That said, if you're dreaming of one last fling before you settle back into old age, this chapter in particular will help you decide if you're ready now for a great escape, if you should wait a few years, or if a vacation is all you really need to brighten your spirits.

> *We kept waiting until everything was wrapped up.*
> *But it never is, so finally we just did it. We were fortunate*
> *because we had family here to help the transition.*
>
> —Treasa, 39, Algarve, Portugal

Four Essential Factors to Consider Before Running Away

Your Personality

Are you cut out to live in another culture? Be honest now. You could simply be bored with your job, and anything that smacks of not working may sound good to you. Consider if you'd be happy with the new challenge of living overseas, or if you might simply need to make changes in your everyday life, without taking such drastic measures.

Major corporations know that some people just don't function well overseas. When they are planning to transfer employees overseas, they must take this into consideration. It's expensive for a corporation to transfer people who won't succeed overseas, both in money and wasted productivity. In fact, one moving company representative estimates it costs $350,000 to $500,000 to transfer someone overseas for a corporation. Don't panic: it won't cost you anywhere near that. This figure includes increased salary, higher rents for people moving to expensive large cities, and private school for their children. The early retiree or person switching to a semiretired lifestyle won't require these expensive extras.

However, just as a corporation must be sure their employees will function well overseas, you should apply the same consideration to yourself to ensure that you make this extensive life change successfully.

If you're leaving a job and a home, and spending your own money on this adventure, it's all the more important to find out—before you make the move—if you'll really be happy with this massive change.

Brenda Bellon of Prudential Intercultural, a firm that specializes in preparing corporate employees for their moves overseas, performs an Overseas Assessment Inventory of potential expatriates, including the spouse. The test checks the attributes essential to successful cross-cultural adjustment. "No one is perfect," she says, "but knowing where people fall on the scale helps determine where they can improve before they leave for overseas."

One of the most important aspects the test checks for is the person's ability to accept different ways of life and adapt to them, rather than insisting that their way is the only way. The person should enjoy the process of discovery, and Ms. Bellon thinks that a sense of humor is an asset: "Not as in telling jokes, but in finding the fun in situations."

You don't need to have a formal test as a corporate employee might, but do a fast check to see where your mind is . . . and prepare yourself to open it.

The New Culture
The biggest shocks to the system when you move to a new culture are not the major changes, but the small things. That blankety blank bathroom has no shower and that small bathtub is a slippery little devil to boot. Then you discover the local bookstore doesn't stock English-language paperbacks, and you're dying for a good mystery. You miss cheeseburgers or the convenience of having pizza delivered on a rainy night.

Every overseas culture will offer small challenges like these, as well as larger ones, such as a new language. If the culture is vastly different, make sure that it's one you would enjoy discovering. If you really don't want to try a new language, choose a country where you know the language. Even if it confuses you when that Brit tells you to put something other than a sock in your "boot," at least you'll know enough of the language to ask what they're talking about.

The language may be the same in English-speaking countries, but the customs will be different. You must be willing to try a new lifestyle on for size and adapt to it. If you compare your new country to the United States, you'll only succeed in making yourself miserable and the people around you frustrated, at best, or irritated, at worst. Your lifestyle will change, and that's the whole point—or else you might as well stay at home.

I recognize that things will be different but weigh the gains far ahead
of the few sacrifices, not counting moving away from friends and family, of course.
But even that is manageable if you make your visits home count.

—Ben, 40, Caracas, Venezuela

Your Family

If you're married, your spouse must be on the same track as you are. Do you both agree on the adventure? Or is one of you more eager than the other? Even if one is definitely more excited by the prospect, be sure the other one is still happy about the move. One woman had dreamed for years of painting in Paris. When her husband reached a point at which he could break away from his business in Texas, they decided to go. Though her husband wasn't as passionate about the move as she was, he was a willing participant.

If you're taking a child, you must consider carefully how that child will adapt. Young children will often adapt well. In fact, they will quickly surpass the parents in making friends through school and learning a new language.

However, an older child or teenager may be confused or frightened by the changes, especially one who's forced to leave friends in the middle of high school. In the latter case, you might be better off waiting until your child goes to college.

You're fortunate if you still have your parents at midlife, but they are also a responsibility if they are very elderly or ill. Some people find support systems and leave their parents. Some take their parents with them. You may even find this to be a preferable and cost-saving alternative to finding care for your parents in the States. In some countries, such as Mexico or Portugal, it may be vastly less expensive to find good household help to care for an elderly parent.

Friends of ours are making this decision now. He's in their new home in the French countryside; she's still in the States while her ninety-year-old mama decides whether to move overseas with them or stay in the States alone. These are tough, sometimes heart-wrenching decisions. Whether you will decide to leave while you have these responsibilities depends on you, your parents, and whether or not you have other family or caregivers nearby.

Our families think we have lost our minds but since they were
already on the West Coast and we were on the East, we didn't see them often.
I don't know what difference a little longer plane flight makes.

—Claire, 45, Algarve, Portugal

Your Finances

We once met an American writer who was being fed gratis thanks to the generosity of a French café owner until his financial situation turned around. We don't suggest you do anything that will get you in this fix (even if the food was very good in this café overlooking the Seine!). After you read more of this book, figure out a way to have your adventure and eat too. It can be done. This is just a matter of planning to save more and spend less.

Most of us runaways have found ways to live pleasantly within our means. We saved and figured out ways to cut the costs once we were settled in our new homes. Living as an expatriate means giving up a bit materially, but believe me, I haven't met a long-time expat who minds. The adventure is well worth giving up an extra here and there.

> *Do it. If it doesn't work out, you can always go home.*
> —Peter, 60, Saint Senoch, France

Good Times to Run Away

Certain times in life and certain situations are better than others for running away—or at least easier. These are the times where your life is in flux anyway:

- *Early retirement.* If you've gotten a hefty early retirement package and you're itching to go, then why not?
- *Between jobs.* You're out of work anyway. If you can afford a year break, then now's the time to find yourself a new life.
- *Traditional retirement.* No, you're not too old. Retirement is that much richer when you have new experiences to buoy your spirits.
- *Moving homes/downsizing.* If you'll be selling the house anyway, you may want to take a break before buying another. In our case, we were ready to downsize to cut costs for early retirement. We did it. Except our downsized house is in France.
- *Planning an overseas job.* Even if you don't want to quit work, if you're able to find an overseas position, you can have your adventure and a salary too.
- *A renewed spirit of creativity.* Burnt out and ready to try your hand at art or writing or whatever creative spirit moves you? Give yourself the gift of time with six months, a year, or more to explore new vistas.

> *The seed for our voyage was planted years before our actual departure. As we ventured farther from our home port on the East Coast of the U.S., we expanded our horizons and finally purchased a yacht we felt was up to crossing oceans. We bought her three years before our actual departure. These three years were filled with a myriad of organization plans, such as preparations to retire, sell our home, make sure our adult children were self-sufficient, ready the boat, study the entry requirements for various countries and make sure our own physical plants were in tip-top order.*
> —Sue and Jim, worldwide cruisers

Good Reasons to Sit Still

You should probably scratch any thought of living overseas if (a) you've never watched *National Geographic;* (b) you watched it but asked why they didn't cover those women properly; or (c) you made your parents pick you up at summer camp after one night, and you've never been away from home since.

OK, seriously, there are times when your family may be growing or when the children might have specific needs or problems that can't be handled at a distance. Other reasons not to run away include the following:

• You'll need to deplete your retirement funds to fund living expenses.
• You love your job and your life just the way it is.
• You're a workaholic and wouldn't know what to do with the free time.
• Parents or other family members are ill and need your help.

None of these reasons mean you won't ever be able to run away. The timing just may not be right at the moment. Start planning though. You can still enjoy the pleasure of reading about, preparing for, and imagining your trip. The planning will also make the transition go all the more smoothly when you finally do take off.

I admitted to a friend that I would have to give up some things Americans take for granted in order to live overseas. Her response was "I wouldn't give up one thing to live in a foreign country." Obviously, she was not-for-export.
—Anne, 61, Albufeira, Portugal

You've Decided to Run Away, Now What?

Wait. Yes, even if you've made that exciting decision to try overseas life, the next most important step is to work out a plan. Like the scouts, "be prepared" should be your goal, ensuring that you do all you can to make your adventure a roaring success. This requires waiting a minimum of six months, most likely a year or longer.

It takes longer to run away from home when you're a grown-up with adult responsibilities. It took you twenty years or more to accumulate the life you have now. You can't expect to shed it in a month.

However, just because you're waiting to make the big move, doesn't mean you'll sit twiddling your thumbs. No, not at all. In fact the waiting time is some of the most exciting as you dream, prepare, and anticipate. Remember when you were a kid, waiting and hoping for a birthday present you were sure was coming? This is the adult version. Planning your adventure will give every day more zest as you plan and dream in Technicolor.

The time speeds by, and you need all of it to absorb the information you'll need to gather. In our case, it took us five years from the day we sat in a sidewalk café in France and one of us mused, "Wouldn't it be great to live here for a year?" until we actually came back to live. But when we did, we felt comfortable with the idea and were prepared to enjoy it to the fullest.

What will you do with all this time? Plenty.

Study Destinations

You may already have a general idea of where you'd like to go. But you'll need time to determine one specific area of a country or plan the travel to several different ones. Read about the specific area. Talk to people who've been there. Read travel articles. Rent videos. Read novels set in the area. The Internet is the greatest invention for runaways since backpacks. In travel channels you can talk to people who live overseas or have just returned.

Take a Test Trip

If you've chosen one specific place to live for a year or longer, make a preliminary visit. Of course, if you want to travel around the world, you won't do that. That's the trip itself. But, you should take a trip to some locale comparable to where you'll be going. Especially if you haven't ever gone overseas. The essential thing is to try it yourself. Make sure you're not living someone else's dream or being swayed by some travel writer's effusive prose.

Learn a Language

If you're going to adventure overseas, then try to learn another language. Naturally, you should learn the language for the country where you'll be going, presuming it's different than the one you speak now. Even if you are going to a country where English is widely spoken, you'll have a much better time if you attempt to learn the native language. Besides, if you can't learn even a bit, why would you choose to live in that country?

I've met several expats who didn't learn the native language of the country they're living in yet still manage. But the people who knew a bit before they arrived, then worked at practicing the language, had more fulfilling experiences as a whole than those who thought they'd "pick it up when I get there." As an adult, it takes time to master a language, so give yourself that head start by beginning well before you get on the plane.

Learn the Customs

Language is not the only difference in other countries, of course. The culture and customs will be different. For example, in some countries different hand signals mean different things. You won't want to give offense. Be a cultural ambassador. Learn about your new environment. It will make your life easier once you're there.

Richard Curry from A. C. White moving company in Atlanta says, "I recommend cross-cultural training. The last thing you want to do is spend that money and have a failed relocation."

Read up on the country you've chosen. Learn its geography, weather, typical lifestyles, social structure, and the practical details of daily life. Of course, you can't discover everything without living there, and that's the point of having this adventure, but do try to get a feel for the culture before you choose your destination.

Talk to people who've been there, either as visitors or residents. If you can find a cross-cultural training course, consider taking it. Believe me, there will always be surprises, but when you know what to expect in general, you're better able to weather a new culture and enjoy the experience.

Many of my friends thought we were crazy for leaving the easy
American way of life where everything works and trading it for hour-long
lines in banks, potholes the size of moon craters, water shortages and electrical
failures. They don't realize that people in Venezuela know how to live
and enjoy everyday life. People make time to visit friends, go out
everyday, and they don't worry . . . until tomorrow!
—Maria Eugenia, 36, Caracas, Venezuela

Network Internationally
Once you decide to run away, make your wishes known far and wide—unless, of course, your boss will hear about it! Once you start spreading the word, you'll be surprised how many people will respond with information or friends to look up overseas. They'll provide the on-site information you need to feel comfortable and learn insider tips on the country and culture you're headed towards.

Arrange Home and Finances
Fixing up your house to sell or rent it for the best price takes time. So does deciding what to do with your car, furniture, and all the other baggage of life. You'll need to review your financial picture with your accountant and other advisors to determine your "running away" budget.

Initial decisions—for example, whether to rent or sell the house—often change from one week to the next, as new input comes in. Ensure that you make well-considered decisions by not rushing them.

Visualize Your New Life
Sports trainers often tell their athletes to imagine the moment of hitting the ball or making the big play. After you've read enough and seen the area you want, run through in your mind what it will be like there. Read novels and nonfiction about the country and its culture to understand its background.

Then imagine what you will do with your days. Will you take art lessons? Learn to cook native dishes? How will you make friends? Having a mental plan and making lists galore will give your new life structure, so you won't feel so adrift when you move.

Be prepared for the fact that a long-term stay is different than a vacation. You'll have a real life overseas, complete with dentist visits, haircuts, and trips to the vet with the dog. It will just be more interesting—all of it.

> *Don't let fear or the Nay-Sayers or the Gertie Glooms dissuade you.*
> *Do your homework, then go for it! Portugal (or France or Argentina or*
> *Fiji) is not Mars. You can go back if it doesn't work out.*
> —Anne, 61, Albufeira, Portugal

Plan Your Reentry
It sounds crazy to plan coming back before you've even left, doesn't it? But that's exactly what you should do. I'm not saying you should know exactly where and when you'll return. But you should know what the options will be for a return. It will make it easier to decide what to do with your home and possessions. If you plan to return to the same city, you may want to rent your house so it will be there later, growing in equity and value. However, if you plan to move to a smaller home anyway, you may want to sell your home to avoid concern over it.

TEST YOURSELF: WILL YOU MAKE A GOOD RUNAWAY?

Are you interested in learning more about other cultures?

Are you willing to learn a new language?

Are you interested in meeting new people and learning about them?

Are you adaptable when it comes to finding new interests and activities?

Do you have confidence in your ability to adapt to a new culture?

Are you able to handle stress?

Do you have a good sense of humor (not jokewise, but able to find fun in situations)?

Are you in good health?

Are you accepting of other people's values and beliefs?

Are you flexible and willing to adapt to new conditions?

If married, do you and your spouse communicate well?

Are you patient?

Do you enjoy trying new food and drink?

Are you willing to adapt to different living conditions?

Do you feel comfortable trying new things?

Do you have a sense of adventure?

Logistically, can you free yourself at this time?

How did you do? If you got a perfect score, all yeses, you're probably already overseas. If you answered with mostly yes answers, then see where you're uncomfortable and if you still care to try the adventure (for example, if you're not willing to learn a new language, you can still try an English-speaking area). If you answered no to everything, give this book to a friend!

3

Where in the World
Will You Go?

The best runaways understand that it's not enough to run away. You must be running toward something. There are so many possibilities! Life opens up when you have new frontiers to explore. It's exciting to plan where you will go and what you will do when you get there. And, yes, you may be surprised that you can live many places on even a limited income—and often you may even be able to afford a better lifestyle than you could in the States. Charles Longino, a gerontologist at Wake Forest University, commented in the *International Herald Tribune:* "There is, and will be, a continued attraction of retirees to overseas retirement places, where on the same income you can afford a maid and some other things you can't have here."

Obviously, this accounts for the large numbers of retirees who have chosen destinations such as Mexico, where they can live more successfully on Social Security.

Though this book is about planning the adventure and not destinations per se, this chapter provides some things to consider before you make a move. Plus, just for the fun of it, you'll find a few destinations that other Americans have found to their liking. Start dreaming with them.

*When I retired I wanted to see more of Europe. It made better
sense to leave New Jersey, save the six-hour flight time, and move to Europe.*
—Dick, 52, Algarve, Portugal

FACTORS AFFECTING YOUR PLANS

Don't select a location for your adventure simply because someone else thinks it's the most wonderful place on earth. We're all individuals, and the whole point of being an authentic overseas adventurer is to find your own idea of paradise. After all, one man's dream of an idyll on the beach in the South Seas could be another's idea of stultifying inactivity. Or, the exciting city life of London or Paris may be too much traffic for the person looking for a quieter way of life. Take a wide range of factors into consideration. Below are some of the more important ones.

Travel or a New Home Base?
The first consideration is whether you want to travel from one place to another or settle on a new home base. If traveling, you'll need greater reserves of both flexibility and money. Travel is expensive no matter where you are, for hotels, transportation, and meals in restaurants. There are ways around this, of course. You could camp or stay in youth hostels or arrange for a series of home exchanges.

The alternative is to find a home base overseas. This will tie you to one location, but that's also its advantage. You'll have a regular place where you can return for mail and relax from the travel pressures, yet you can easily explore from there if you like.

*Our desire was not primarily to live overseas, but to live
on the seas and circumnavigate the globe. In so doing we have had the
opportunity to visit 42 countries over the five-year period.*
—Sue and Jim, worldwide cruisers

Financial Facts of Life
I'm optimistic that someone who really wants an adventure overseas can eventually figure out a way to fund it. At the same time, you must fine-tune your adventure to what you can afford. As already mentioned, constant travel sends your money flying. An affordable base lets you husband your costs a bit by shopping at local markets, eating more meals at home, and having a long-term lease with lower overall costs than tourist hotels.

Also, if you need to work, there's no choice; you'll need a base. Even if you plan to simply do odd jobs, you need to build contacts and stay in one spot long enough to at least accumulate a stash for your next move (for more about finances, see chapter 4, "How to Pay for Your Getaway").

Consider the cost of living at your destination. If you're losing sleep over whether you can afford to pay the heat in winter, you won't be enjoying yourself living abroad. For information on how costs compare you can check statistics from publications, such as the State Department's *Indexes of Living Costs Abroad*, at your local library.

Quarterly statistics show the relative costs indexed for various locations around the world as compared to the United States. These figures are used by many private companies to adjust pay of American employees abroad, but you can use them to determine relative costs in locations you may be considering.

You can compare costs in cities through the "Cost of Living of United Nations Personnel in Selected Cities" section from the United Nations' *Monthly Bulletin of Statistics*. In 1996 the figures showed that on a scale of 100, Paris rates 119, Rome 104, Caracas 90, Washington 92, Geneva 148, Athens 92.

Cities in general are more costly than living in the countryside, so remember that as you gather your information. In addition, some cost-of-living statistics are only as valid for real life as the system used for gathering them. I've found that some statistics may include the cost of items irrelevant to your chosen lifestyle. On the other hand, be aware that inflation and fluctuating exchange rates can affect costs of living, so use the most up-to-date information you can find or adjust. Happily the U.S. dollar has strengthened lately, giving Americans more buying power in many places overseas.

Some countries are truly more expensive places to live than others, but your actual costs will depend on how you manage your own budget and the style of life you choose. One advantage of moving far from home is that preconceived notions can be jettisoned along with your old lifestyle. Though we once lived in Detroit, new car capital of the United States, now our neighbors could care less what we drive, as long as it doesn't block their gate.

One thing that I don't miss is winter. Caracas is springlike with typical highs of 84–86 and lows of 65–66, except December and January, with lows in the high 50s. There is something called the "rainy season," which after a couple of years I figured out means those months when it can, and sometimes does, rain. The rest of the year the northern third of the country is very dry. That keeps the humidity and insect levels down and comfort levels up—at least as long as the beer is cold!
—Ben, 40, Caracas, Venezuela

Weather

One of the main attractions for some older Americans who move overseas is a temperate year-round environment. That's one reason Mexico and the Caribbean come to mind when many people think of paradise. However, many expats dream of England and Ireland, which are not exactly known for their wonderful climes. Your choice is also a matter of comparison between where you lived in the States and where you want to live. One expat from

Minneapolis, now in France's Loire Valley, brags about the warmth in winter, while the ex-Atlantan who lives nearby turns the heat up in her house.

Culture/Language
If you're eager to live in another country, assuming it's not English-speaking, then you must apply yourself to learn enough of that country's language to be polite and survive on a daily basis. Start this while still in the planning stages in the United States.

The same is true of a country's culture. Your knowledge of another country (notice I don't say foreign; they aren't the foreigners when you're there!) doesn't stop with knowing the language. Culture is part of the fabric of everyday life. To use an example from my locale in France, people say "*bonjour*" on entering and "*au revoir*" on leaving the small shops. To not do so is impolite because the shops are owned by local people and it's rather like entering their domain. An expat who understands this would follow local custom and be more readily welcomed.

Access to Health Care
A practical matter, but vital, is access to good doctors, dentists, and hospital care—perhaps even those that speak English. This will be especially relevant if you have a medical condition that requires monitoring on a regular basis.

Rugged Individualist or Social Butterfly
Being on the go constantly is an independent way of seeing the world. This may be for you if you want to see many areas in short spurts and don't need to put down roots.

The alternative is to have a home base overseas, which allows you to settle in and become part of the community. You'll meet the butcher, the baker, and the candlestick maker . . . not to mention other expats and the lady next-door. You can take language classes, cooking classes, or art lessons.

Also consider whether you want to experience an extremely different culture in which you are one of the few Americans. Or would you be happier in an area with several other expats for companionship?

> *The Italian people were really nice, but the infrastructure was so messed up we couldn't get anything done. Phones were bad. And no one could give us a bill. When we left, we had to chase down the garageman to pay him.*
> —Craig, 52, France (formerly Italy)

Energy Level
When you first start out you think you want to see it all, do it all. But being on the road constantly can be exhausting. Imagine trying to cram four museums into a day. You can't enjoy them all.

Most people soon discover that they eventually want a familiar place to which they can return. It's a nesting instinct, stronger in some than in others. Only you know how strong this instinct is in you. But be prepared. Some people think they want complete and utter freedom, then find that it's a bit too much of a good thing. Don't worry if you suddenly want to settle down somewhere.

RESEARCHING LOCATIONS AROUND THE WORLD

How in heaven's name do you know what it's like on the Greek coast or in an Irish country cottage? You don't. But careful research will provide enough input to narrow your choices. Then you visit the locations before you move there permanently.

Review your choices and base your final decision on careful consideration of the most important factors. Here are a few ways to uncover the information you need and get a solid feel for the destinations you're considering.

Read All About It
Your local library, bookstores, and your friends' bookshelves are the first stop. Gather together all the books you can and read up about the areas you're considering.

Read a range of materials, some for general overviews of the culture to see how you'd fit in and like it, others for specifics that will help you plan expenses, or living accommodations, for example.

Be careful to pick out the most current books. A word of warning: Some guidebooks are originally written in England and are often good if you're planning a hiatus in Europe because, after all, the Brits are closer to the Continent than Americans and are frequently much more knowledgeable about it. However, by the time these books are purchased by a publisher in the United States and find their way to the stores, they may be several years older than some of the American books. This may not matter if you're reading for general impressions. But if you're relying on prices for apartments or transportation, be sure you have the most up-to-date materials.

Check the library and video rental store for travel videos. And watch the public TV channels for specials on areas of the world that you're interested in.

Write for Specifics
For the most current information on a specific location, write the tourist boards and enclose an International Reply Coupon (found at your local post office), which will provide return postage for your information.

You'll find some recommended books in the bibliography at the back of this book, which will start you off on the right foot.

Find It on the Web

It's called the "World Wide Web" for good reason. You can connect to virtually any place you want to go on the Internet. If you have access to it, use it to research destinations and find new friends in those locations (yes, even before you move there).

You say you don't know anyone in Italy or Greece or any other destination you're interested in visiting? Different Internet services offer different options, but you can often search using the name of the country and the town or location where you want to live. You can find members of that service who live there, then send messages.

For more specifics on how to use the Web to research or keep in touch overseas, see chapter 17, "The Internet Advantage."

> *There's a lot to be said for a country that, with a population*
> *of even now not more than 22 million, is second only to the U.S.*
> *in number of winners of the Miss Universe contest.*
> —Ben, 40, Caracas, Venezuela

Do Some Personal Networking

Talk to anyone you can think of about your plans. You'll pick up tidbits of information in the strangest places. The friend you play bridge with has a cousin whose son just got back from an exchange program in Italy. Your hairdresser's best friend's parents are now spending the winter in Mexico. The lady sending a package to France in the Pak 'n' Mail is actually moving there next month. (The latter happened to me and she now lives an hour away in the Loire Valley!)

Make a Trial Visit

Before you sell the family homestead to set out for parts unknown, know the parts you're heading toward. Visit the area at least once—or more—before you chuck everything. You may decide that you don't like that particular location, but you would like to try another area. You may even decide that a vacation was all you really needed or that you just aren't cut out for living overseas. You found out you like American-style showers and driving your car from store to store and central heating. You've at least learned something. You may even appreciate that old life you wanted to run away from before.

> *We loved Europe, having lived in England many years ago for work.*
> *We always longed to return to this side of the Pond. It's slightly exotic. It's*
> *challenging. And it's a helluva lot warmer than Massachusetts!*
> —Anne, 61, Albufeira, Portugal

RATE YOUR DESTINATION

Consider these factors when determining your ideal spot for a long-term adventure or overseas retirement.

Economic
• How does the cost of living compare to the United States?
• What are the taxes?
• Can you buy and sell property, invest, or set up a business in the location?
• Can you work in the country if you want to?
• How does housing compare?

Environmental
• Is the climate to your liking?
• Are there cleanliness or water-quality problems you can't deal with?
• Can you count on the telephone and mail services?

Stability
• Is the government stable?
• Are there special problems with crime or violence?
• As a foreigner, will you feel comfortable in this location?

Health Care
• What is the availability of quality medical, hospital, and dental services?
• And are they affordable?
• Can you purchase medical insurance at a reasonable rate?

Cultural
• Are there museums, libraries, theaters?
• What about movie theaters (in English or a foreign language)?
• Are there sports activities?
• Do you have access to television and radio?
• Is shopping nearby?
• Is there a different language, and if so, are you willing to learn it?
• Are the local people friendly toward Americans?

Travel
• How easy is it to travel back to the States for visits?
• Is the area close to an international airport or a good road system if you want to travel or return home for visits?
• Can friends visit you easily? (This is a plus or minus depending on your wish to entertain!)
• Is there a good internal transportation system—buses, trains, airlines, roads?

*I've traveled all over. Now I'm content settling down
with my garden, art, and cuisine, and they're all superb here.*

—Frances, 59, Antibes, France

WHERE HAVE YOU DREAMED OF GOING?

Have you always wanted to study opera in Italy? Paint in Provence? Your destination is a highly personal decision, but with study and some intro-spection you'll arrive at a favorite. Or, you may want to travel to several areas. Our own choice was to rent a house in France as a base for four months in Europe, intending to move to lower-cost Mexico later. Instead we discovered that we could afford to live in the French countryside and bought a small home nearby (yes, that nesting instinct really took hold).

Americans Are Everywhere

According to the Bureau of Consular Affairs, American expatriates can be found from Albania to Zimbabwe. More than three million by the official count, but keep in mind that these numbers are much lower than the actual numbers, since not all Americans living abroad report their presence to the consulate.

Here are a few of the destinations and the number of Americans living there.

COUNTRY	NO. OF AMERICANS (as reported to consulate)	COUNTRY	NO. OF AMERICANS (as reported to consulate)
Albania	2,200	Ireland	36,000
Argentina	900	Italy	146,100
Australia	63,800	Japan	66,316
Bahamas	7,600	Mexico	619,147
Belgium	31,614	Portugal	9,045
Bermuda	4,250	Spain	62,698
Canada	626,585	Switzerland	32,600
Costa Rica	19,000	United Kingdom	
France	86,037	(England, Ireland, Scotland)	216,000
Greece	82,500	Venezuela	23,425

A FEW DREAM DESTINATIONS

Each country offers its own unique set of characteristics and related benefits, whether it's sunny weather, wonderful cuisine, tropical beaches, scenic mountains, or fascinating culture. Though a complete listing can't be included, here are some popular destinations.

France. The world's top tourist destination is also a prime place to live for those who love good food, culture, and a location centrally located for travel to other areas of Europe. France can be expensive, but provided you're will-ing to find the small village that's off the tourist track, it can also be afford-able. Consider Paris or the Côte d'Azur only if you've just won the lottery.

If you go to Mexico for one of those "Wonder Weekends," you won't get it. To savor Mexico, you must stay awhile, and then you're hooked. We don't know what it is. The climate? The warmth of the people? The fact that it is truly the last Great Travel Bargain?
—Betts, 74, Mexico

Mexico. One of the winners for low cost, Mexico is a favorite of American expatriates. Several areas are filled with English speakers. Over 46,000 of them live near Guadalajara and nearby Lake Chapala alone. They offer a ready base of friendship and tips, plus they've already prepared the way with the comforts that you may be used to. The area's culture is fascinating, filled with fine pottery and interesting villages to explore.

Mexico, however, is a third-world country so be prepared to adapt your way of eating and drinking (though most expats here say it rapidly becomes second nature to keep bottled drinking water handy). The other negative has surfaced recently with internal troubles in some areas of the country, though not where most retirees have chosen to settle.

The cost of living is so low in Mexico that it's actually possible to live on Social Security there. A person can be comfortable on $12,000 to $15,000 a year, including domestic help.

We had lived in Britain for Bob's work and liked Europe. But we wanted a warmer area, so we investigated Italy, Spain, Portugal. The last place we checked was Portugal and it happened to be February with the almond blossoms in bloom. That did it. We decided to stay.
—Anne, 61, Albufeira, Portugal

Portugal. Very few Americans have discovered this country, though the British and Germans have. In the Algarve you'll find that English is spoken most places. The trade-off in the Algarve is the large number of tourists, though there's still enough of the native culture in the off-season to explore. The expats I met actually prefer the winter, when they have the place to themselves, as opposed to August's vacation crowds.

It is possible to live cheaply or work "underground" or live poshly in one of the new golf communities. For greener acres than the dry Algarve in summer, the north of Portugal is less inundated by tourists and, therefore, also less costly. It can also be more interesting to operate within the true Portuguese culture, but you'll have to learn Portuguese, which is a particularly difficult language.

Italy. Many Americans rhapsodize over the joys of Italy, which range from Tuscany, with its lovely old villas, wine, and access to some of the most beautiful cities in the country, such as Florence and Venice, to the vibrancy of Rome or Milan. What begins as a love of the country for vacations, turns into settling there, whether in a city or a quiet village.

Costa Rica. Rain forests and friendly people, low cost and warmth year-round are some of the benefits of living in Costa Rica. Though a bit off the beaten path, and not for restless New Yorkers, for people who dream of an easy, tropical lifestyle, Costa Rica may be the choice.

England. The language may be the same as that spoken by North Americans, but the culture is very different. Many people appreciate England's charms, though many others are champing at the bit to leave due to the infamous weather (in fact, we have several Brit friends now in France). The countryside, however, is lovely, and with a cozy fire and afternoon teas, England may suit you just fine.

Ireland. The people know how to spin a tale in this land of literary greatness. The country is lush and green (with the weather, there's a reason), and the people are hospitable. There are charms, to be sure, in Ireland, and monetary incentives as well. Housing, except in Dublin, is reasonable. Artists and writers enjoy tax-free living, and retirees get tax breaks. Residents are eligible for the national health program, and those over sixty-five can get a travel card for free bus and train travel.

Caribbean. There are so many different islands you could travel to, and you can't beat the weather if you like it warm year-round.

Australia. From modern cities like contemporary Sydney (site of the 2000 summer Olympic games), to coastal areas including the Great Barrier Reef, to the rough 'n' ready outback, Australia is a dynamic young country ready for settlers. The most sparsely populated of all inhabited continents affords nature lovers the space to roam and a chance to enjoy flora and fauna that's unique in the world—plus a tropical to temperate climate (though seasons are reversed) for a superb outdoor lifestyle.

> When we lived in England it was a tremendous wrench for me.
> My husband chose a small village and I'm a city person. Many years
> later, after he died, I came here. It's been 22 years, and I still love it. But I
> know that not everyone would. If you can live with making plans for the
> day and then having everything go differently, then you can live here!
> —Judy, 62, Athens, Greece

Greece. The country can be leisurely and laid-back on a hidden beach or loudly crowded during tourist season in Athens. The Greek isles offer scenic but harsh landscapes and brilliant sun, rich archaeological treasures, and centuries of history. This is heaven on earth for those who are entranced by it, though quite the opposite for those who insist upon modern efficiencies.

Spain. Ah, sunny sea coasts, beautiful Barcelona and Seville and mighty Madrid—add Spanish wines and tapas in the late afternoon, and Spain is paradise for Americans who love the culture. Check the weather though. Madrid, for example, is hot and dry in the summer. Too hot, in fact, for many people's tastes. Most expats head for the seacoasts, east and south of Barcelona.

South Africa. Exotic, scenic, and pleasantly temperate, South Africa is enjoying a resurgence since the fall of apartheid, particularly among African-Americans who are interested in discovering their heritage. The country is still undergoing growing pains, however. Communication is not a problem since the official languages are both English and Afrikaans (a variety of Dutch).

New Zealand. A temperate climate, beautiful coastlines, scenic mountains, and lush flora make New Zealand a natural for anyone who loves the outdoors, and its isolation makes it a haven for independent souls. Southeast of Australia, New Zealand is composed of two large islands, North Island and South Island, plus a range of smaller ones, so water sports abound. The country is prosperous and residents benefit from a high standard for social services. Anyone phobic about learning a new language can rest easy since English prevails.

Japan. The language may provide some difficulties, but language also offers an entree for English speakers who want to work in Japan. English teachers are in demand for businesses and schools, so your native language may provide the means of working here. Outside of work, enjoy the thrill of an ancient heritage and culture, which exudes politeness, cleanliness, and a refreshingly low crime rate.

Do the above descriptions whet your appetite to find out more? I hope so. There are countless other destinations to explore and you can uncover specific and in-depth details from countless sources. Don't leave it to me. Study up on those countries that intrigue you.

4

How to Pay for Your Getaway

RICHES ARE CHIEFLY
GOOD BECAUSE THEY GIVE US TIME.
—Charles Lamb

If we were all rich as Rockefellers, running away would not be a problem. I assume, not being one, that the jet-setters of the world simply keep a few homes handy anywhere they want to be. If this is you, then forget this book and call a real estate agent.

However, at midlife the money issue is probably your number one concern when deciding to run away from home. None of us wants to spend our later years as bag ladies (or bag men) because we spent our retirement funds too freely while still in our forties, fifties, or sixties.

Happily, you may discover that your concerns about not having enough money to plan a long-term adventure may result from misinformation, false expectations, or fear of the unknown. A few years back, my husband and I never dreamed that we could afford life abroad, since we equated it with *Lifestyles of the Rich and Famous*. A little investigation uncovered the fact that real people live overseas too, and many times less expensively than in the States.

If you want to get more out of your life, consider all the possibilities, examine the reality of your assets, and determine what you'll need for a sojourn overseas. You may find that you can afford to begin an adventure now. Even if you fall short, there are ways to save or scale back that will eventually enable you to enjoy the lifestyle overseas.

How Much Do You *Really* Need?

One man's wealth is another man's poverty. You'll have to determine for yourself exactly how much you need to live comfortably—all dependent on factors that include the country you choose, your interests, and the type of lifestyle you require.

I can't presume to offer exact numbers. In any case, I'm not a financial advisor. I do, however, know methods for determining expenses overseas that have worked for us and other runaways. These methods will help you estimate your monthly expenses and cut costs. When all is said and done, you may discover that you already have more, or need less, than you think you do.

From the perspective of our home in the French countryside, but with an American's background of "bigger is better," it's clear that most of us have spent our lives trying to make more money. A French friend calls it "*vivre pour travailler*," or "living to work." What you want, if you're seriously interested in running away from home, is the opposite. You must work to live in a way that gives you joy, not just more material objects. Along the way, you'll develop a more balanced perspective on money. Use it to provide the freedom and life experiences that enrich your life, not as an end in itself. (Incidentally, one book that's a great inspiration and guide along this score is *Your Money or Your Life*, by Joe Dominguez and Vicki Robin.)

Once you think of money as a tool, not a goal, you'll discover that the cost of something is not always proportional to the pleasure it provides. Right now, we're having ten times more fun on half the money we used to spend in the States. The same can be said of half the friends we have overseas. Unquestionably, it's possible to live better abroad, if you're willing to adjust your expectations and adapt. You, too, may find that you already have the resources for an adventure overseas.

Gain Freedom with Downsizing

The downsizing I recommend has nothing to do with the corporate downsizing that took a lot of midlife and middle-income people by surprise, leaving them out of work in the early nineties. The downsizing I want you to consider is voluntary downsizing by which you maneuver yourself into position to get off the treadmill and discover new horizons.

You may think, "Oh, I can't live without a new car every two years." If you can afford it, more power to you. But material wealth is not relevant when you're living an overseas adventure filled with the joys of discovery. Once you're beyond the thirst for more material things, you'll discover that you enjoy making do and doing for yourself—especially when it provides the freedom you've been wanting to write or hike, visit great museums, or just sleep on a sunny beach. But how much is enough?

A Richer Life for Less

A host of financial advisors claim that a person needs 70 to 80 percent of their working income to retire. Whether or not you're of actual retirement age, running away may require quitting work. If so, use this figure as a starting point. Keep in mind, however, that this figure may be too low by a long shot or even too high. (If you've already got too much, don't complain, just get going!)

Start with some honest soul-searching. You can't live on 70 to 80 percent of your working income if you plan to spend more money once you have time to travel, eat out, shop—and if you insist on all the extra conveniences we Americans take for granted. Insisting on luxury, however, can delay your capturing the prize of enjoying *life* instead of *belongings*. Setting new priorities can cut costs.

You won't need the 70 to 80 percent of what you're living on now if you intend to simplify or live in a less expensive locale. Running away provides the ideal opportunity to free yourself from old constraints and expenses. No more three-piece suits and silk ties; shorts do just fine on a Greek isle. No need for a Mercedes to impress the neighbors when you can take the Mercedes bus for the equivalent of a few dollars (with TV and comfy seats!) through central Mexico's colonial villages. And why pay that steep mortgage for a huge house your kids have left, when you can get a smaller, paid-for home near a sunny Portuguese beach?

Your ability to enjoy life while cutting costs depends on your plans, interests, and personality. Think about the type of place you want to visit or live in long term. Do you dream of running away to a country cottage in Ireland? Do you want to learn Italian in a villa in Tuscany? Will you work to supplement your savings or simply lower your lifestyle to cut all ties with the corporate world? All these decisions impact where you'll live and your actual costs.

Location Counts

Some places naturally cost less to live than others. When you're working, you don't have a choice, since you must live where the jobs are. But when you run away, you can live outside expensive cities or choose a country where your dollars give you an advantage. Mexico, for example, is the choice of many U.S. expats and retirees. The weather is warm and sunny most of the year, and you can live nicely on as little as $12,000 year.

The specific area of a country, even a generally expensive one, makes a big difference, too. Paris is as costly as it is beautiful. But in the French countryside, countless expats own farmhouses that they're renovating for peanuts. Some friends of ours paid about $30,000 for their place, which now has three bedrooms, a bath, kitchen, living room—with the study and other rooms still under renovation. Of course, they're handy and find joy in keeping costs down by being creative in their use of local materials, some even found for free, and doing most of the work themselves. The female half, however, did comment that, if she'd known better, she would have worked on the house while living somewhere else at first. Borrowing the neighbor's "loo" while waiting for plumbing to be installed was not her favorite pastime!

Debt Is a Four-Letter Word

Don't even think of running away until you are free from debt. Pay off your charge cards and any other bills, with the one exception being your home if, and only if, you are able to rent it for more than the mortgage costs.

One Pennsylvania educator and his wife, who regularly disappear for several months overseas, carry this to the extreme of paying several bills in advance, such as medical insurance, to avoid worrying that it may be canceled if they miss the bill. We learned from them. Not only did we pay off our charge cards, we saved enough to prepay our home mortgage, rent overseas, and health insurance for the first three months we were gone. It was wonderfully liberating to begin the adventure with no bills for the first time in over twenty years.

WHERE WILL YOU GET THE MONEY?

Finding the cash to run away requires using what you already have intelligently and saving for what you still need. Combine some of the following methods to reach your goal.

Investment Income

Any investments are grist for use on your adventure. Determine which ones you could use as income, i.e., interest or dividends, or even a limited amount of capital, for the length of time you intend to be gone. If you're under retirement age, however, don't use your IRA or other tax-advantaged investments that come with steep penalties for withdrawal or that you'll later need for retirement.

Runaway Funds from Your Home

If you own your own home, it can help fund your adventure. Renting it for more than your mortgage payment and other costs provides regular monthly income. Consider, however, that you will still be responsible for maintaining the home in case the furnace goes or the roof leaks. Just when we decided to stay overseas longer than a year and incurred moving expenses, our renter announced that the water heater had gone bad, and we had to add that to the list of payments. On the whole though, we've been pleased with our rental experience; we intend to sell the house eventually, to rid ourselves of the problems of managing real estate from overseas.

If you sell your home, the equity in it can be invested. Use the interest on the principal to provide income each month. For example, an equity of $100,000, invested at 8 percent simple interest provides $8,000 a year income, or $667 a month. That pays the rent on an apartment in Italy or a house with pool and maid in Mexico!

A Paying Job

The younger you are when you begin your adventure, the more you must consider the possibility of earning some money to supplement retirement savings. Having income from work will help you preserve and add to your retirement stash, so it will grow to keep up with inflation and, hopefully, surpass it. Working, even part-time, will also help you pay for a longer adventure. However, picking grapes in a French vineyard, romantic as it sounds when you're twenty, might not be your aching back's choice at fifty.

When we began our own sabbatical, we planned for fifteen months away. That was the amount of time we could afford if we didn't work at all. We would use those fifteen months to explore options. If we found that living costs vastly exceeded our savings, we had a backup plan to move to a less expensive locale. As things turned out, we discovered an inexpensive area of France to live, a small house we could afford, and some of my writing clients stuck with me via the Internet. So we're still here.

We're able to live overseas on a New York state teacher's retirement salary plus Social Security. When we first came down, the cost of living was great. You could go out to dinner for less than $5, but now this country's going through difficult times. A pound of ham is more than $6 and rents are over $1,000 a month. Thank goodness we have our house!
—Susan, 65, Venezuela

Social Security

Over a half million people living outside the United States receive monthly federal benefits payments. Some people take them as early as age sixty-two, to help fund their excursion.

The good news is this extra income can help finance an adventure at sixty-two. The bad news is, taking Social Security early reduces your monthly payment for as long as you live. In some cases, you may figure the difference is worth it, since you'll enjoy the freedom sooner. Several expats mentioned that their parents died young, and they themselves had decided to retire overseas early to ensure they'd have time to enjoy it.

Calculate the exact difference and determine what it means for your budget. To estimate your Social Security benefit, call the Social Security Administration at (800) 772-1213 and request your benefit status for both sixty-two and sixty-five. You can then decide if it's worth it to you to take less sooner, or wait for more later.

It's no problem to apply and receive your Social Security check while living outside the United States. Social Security considers "outside" to be anywhere not within the fifty states, District of Columbia, Puerto Rico, U.S. Virgin Islands, Guam, Northern Mariana Islands, or American Samoa.

If you're overseas, apply for Social Security at the nearest American consulate. It may take longer to process your application than in the States, though the process is the same. Our representative requested three months' notice from the office in Paris.

We have my husband's check deposited directly into our U.S. checking account. If you do this, it's easy to take automatic withdrawals overseas, which pop out of the automatic teller machine in the local currency at a favorable exchange rate. The U.S. checking account can also pay stateside expenses, such as credit card bills or your home mortgage.

Your Social Security check can also be mailed to a foreign bank account, which some expats prefer. You'll have to have it exchanged, of course, into the local currency. Another option is to have your check sent to the nearest U.S. consulate; they distribute Social Security checks via the local postal service.

For detailed information, call the Social Security office before leaving the United States and request the pamphlet *Your Social Security Checks While You Are Outside the United States*. This pamphlet is also available through American consulates.

Pension

If you're currently eligible to receive a pension from your job, add this to the money you have available for living expenses. Even if you're too young to draw your pension, ask your benefits office what the amount will be. You can't use it for running away now, of course, but it will be available later and may enable you to use more of your personal savings than someone who has no corporate pension to cushion their later years.

A One-Time Cash Infusion

When you run away you won't need many of the things you're leaving behind. Selling them helps to pay for the initial outlay of cash to set up somewhere else. Remember, however, that anything you sell you may have to buy back if or when you return! Plan for it in your return budget.

Sell your cars if you won't be needing them in the near future. And a garage sale can bring in amazing amounts of cash, depending on how much you determine to get rid of. This is a wonderful opportunity to unclutter your life.

How Much Investment Income Will You Have?

Check with your accountant or investment counselor to see what your average rate of return is on your investments. If you add the equity from a home, you may be surprised how much this adds up to. Let's say, for example, you deposit the equity from selling your house and that comes to $100,000. You add the cash from selling a car for $10,000. And you have savings of about $90,000. Right, I cheated to make this a round number of $200,000. We're just showing an example here. See how that $200,000 will provide cash to add to your Social Security, pension or other income.

$200,000 INVESTED FOR A RETURN OF	6%	7%	8%	9%	10%
Annual income (simple interest)	$12,000	$14,000	$16,000	$18,000	$20,000

You may not be able to live entirely on the interest, but added to other income, it helps make life more comfortable in that sunny Caribbean bungalow.

We did a fairly major sell-off of furniture and belongings in the U.S. to raise money for a year without income. If I were to do it again, I'd do the same. Starting over in a foreign country forces you to adapt quicker. You have to go shopping, negotiate delivery of furniture, etc. You come to terms with different ways of doing things.
—Doug, 43, Basel, Switzerland

Outsmarting the Peril of Inflation

There's one danger in living on your investments while you're under sixty years old: inflation. Even at a relatively minor 3 percent a year, inflation will cut your purchasing power considerably in just a few years. And there's no guarantee that inflation will stay low. At an inflation rate of 6 percent, in five years it would take $134 to buy what $100 will buy today. The younger you are, the greater the threat of inflation.

The solution is to avoid living on all your investment income. Allow your investments to grow by an estimated rate of inflation. The trick is to know what the inflation rate will be in the future. No one can tell you, but recently the figures have approximated 3 to 4 percent in the United States.

The earlier you start your adventure, the more you must allow your money to grow to cover inflation. If you're running away at forty-five without a juicy early retirement package, you must pay for your adventure and contend with inflation for many more years than a person who is sixty-five, getting Social Security, and has fewer years to stretch the savings.

It's safer to avoid relying on the full income from your investments. If, for example, your investments are earning 8 percent and you judge the rate of inflation to be 3 percent, then try living on 5 percent—the difference between earnings and the inflation rate. The untouched 3 percent will continue to grow, increasing your capital to allow for inflation in years to come.

How to Spend a Nest Egg (Without Going Broke)

Money magazine published a chart that shows that the amount of your savings you can spend depends on your expected return on investment, inflation, and how long you need the principal to last.

For example, your nest egg will last twenty years if your portfolio returns an average of 7 percent and you take out 6.5 percent of it the first year, or $13,000 from your $200,000. The table assumes you will increase your withdrawals 4 percent a year to keep pace with inflation.

Years You Want Your Nest Egg to Last	Assuming This Average Annual Return				
	5%	6%	7%	8%	9%
	You Can Use This Much the First Year*				
10 years	10.4%	10.9%	11.3%	11.8%	12.2%
15 years	7.1%	7.6%	8.1%	8.6%	9.1%
20 years	5.5%	6.0%	6.5%	7.0%	7.5%
25 years	4.5%	5.0%	5.5%	6.1%	6.6%
30 years	3.8%	4.3%	4.9%	5.5%	6.1%

*Assuming subsequent withdrawals increase 4 percent a year.

Build a Safety Net

An adventure on a shoestring when you're twenty is one thing. You've got parents to bail you out, you can live on beans, and you've got a lifetime to get back to the "real" world and save for retirement. At midlife no one should blow their retirement stash. You don't have a lot of years to make up for a major financial mistake. So err on the conservative side when planning how much money to take from your savings to finance your runaway plans. Be sure you have enough to allow your money to grow, to counteract inflation years later, and to handle an unexpected emergency. For safety's sake:

• Estimate your initial costs and daily living expenses overseas—then add 20 percent. No matter what, your expenses will go over your estimate. I guarantee it. Better to have estimated high than have your adventure spoiled by panic when an unexpected bill arrives or the exchange rate heads in the wrong direction.

• If you're running away in your forties or fifties, don't touch your retirement funds. These are your protection for old age, and they're tax-deferred. Let them sit there and grow while you use other means to fund your adventure.

• Plan in advance what you will do if you've underestimated costs and start depleting your runaway funds faster than expected. Will you move to a cheaper location? Take a part-time job? Head back to the States and work as a consultant? Knowing before you leave what your fallback position is will give you more confidence in undertaking this move and protect you from unexpected problems.

• If you can't live entirely on your investments or income overseas, be prepared to supplement your income with a transferable skill and know whether or not there's a use for that skill at your destination. For example, if you learn how to teach English as a foreign language, you might pick up some pocket change. Can you sew? Make furniture or refinish antiques? Repair computers? Any or all these skills might provide an interesting way to meet people and supplement your adventure fund.

• Maintain the money needed to tide you over when you return to the States. You'll need cash for housing security deposits or down payments and money to repurchase a car or furnishings you may have sold before you left.

• Finally, maintain an emergency fund to cover six months of expenses and airline tickets home.

5

Costs and How to Cut Them

ALL THINGS ARE POSSIBLE UNTIL THEY ARE
PROVED IMPOSSIBLE—AND EVEN THE IMPOSSIBLE
MAY ONLY BE SO AS OF NOW.
—Pearl Buck

Make up your runaway budget based on interests, age, finances, and willingness to cut costs. Fortunately, you'll discover that expenses overseas are predicated less on "keeping up with the Joneses" and more on necessity and personal desires. Expats tend to be accepting types who are more interested in the adventure and meeting interesting people than in determining whether or not you drive a Mercedes. When we started to rationalize our dented used Citroën in front of one long-time New Zealand expat, he smiled whimsically, "That's an American thing. You don't have to explain because we're all doing the same thing and couldn't care less."

That said, let's look at two categories of expenses you'll incur when you run away from home: (1) start-up costs of getting overseas and getting situated and (2) daily living expenses.

Start-Up Costs

When you run away, you'll incur initial expenses that are necessary to make the transition. You may be able to live, for example, in Mexico on $1,000 a month. But you'll need the money to get there, stay in a hotel while searching for an apartment, rent a car until you're settled, and move your belongings or furnish your lodgings.

Since these are nonrecurring costs you won't have to budget for them monthly. However, you will have to have a lump sum set aside to cover them immediately.

NONRECURRING EXPENSES
Airline tickets   _____

Special shipping expenses   _____
  (luggage, pet container, extra shipping fees)

Car rental and/or car purchase   _____

Moving (movers, boxes)   _____

Classified ads (garage sale, car sale, rent or sell home)   _____

Apartment security deposit   _____

Furnishings overseas   _____
  (appliances or special needs for apartment or home)

Utility set-up   _____
  (fees required to begin service for electric, fuel, phone)

Total $_____

The way of life here allows for cheap yard labor, household help, and errand runners. It felt great to sell every piece of lawn equipment we had before we left!
—Maria Eugenia, 36, Caracas, Venezuela

DAILY LIVING EXPENSES

I debated whether or not to include budget numbers in this book, since there are so many factors that affect how much or how little a person can live on. Within the basic parameters of the area's cost of living, people can be as economical or extravagant as they wish to be.

In Portugal's popular Algarve beach area, for example, I ran across extremely diverse people: from a woman creating a hilltop oasis of simple cottages with her own carpentry skills to a couple working part-time but hoping to quit to a couple enjoying a pool and maid thanks to a healthy retirement package and inheritance. Their budgets ranged from $14,000 a year or less to well over $75,000 a year. Obviously, they'd all give different answers to the question as to how much it takes to live in their area of Portugal.

On the other hand, two questions everyone asks when they first dream of living overseas are "Can I afford it?" and "What does it actually cost?" Unless you're nosy like me, no one ever tells you, since the topic of money, like sex, tends to be off-limits. But everyone wants a starting point, with real figures to mull over, so in an effort to be as helpful as possible, here are a few budget compilations, based on what real people are doing, with any holes filled in by educated guesses based on what I know of the country involved and usual costs. Use these as a base, not a bible, to enable you to see what the possibilities are. Then investigate how you can make your own finances fit in the location you choose.

Let's start with a low-end budget in one of the most economical locations, Mexico, then move to a few other possibilities. These budgets tend to reflect the low to moderate end of the scale for the countries involved. If you've got bunches more money, lucky you.

Year-Round Warmth in Sunny Mexico on $18,000 a Year
This typical couple has reached retirement age but are trying to live mainly on Social Security—something almost impossible in the United States. They didn't want to settle for a boring life in a shoebox apartment in the States. Now they rent a large two-bedroom apartment in colonial Mexico, complete with maid. They socialize with the numerous other expats in the area at cocktail parties and art gallery openings and volunteer at the local English-language library. They use the Mexican bus system, occasionally visiting beach areas or other towns to compare pottery and visit tourist sites.

EXPENSES PER MONTH

Housing	
Rent on two-bedroom apartment	$350
Maid, one day a week	$18
Insurance	$20
Taxes	$12
Utilities	
Electric/gas	$35
Medical	
Health insurance	$40
Life insurance	$180
Doctor/dentist visits	$35
Prescriptions	$20
Communication	
Postage/P.O. Box	$40
Telephone	$25
Groceries	$130
Meals out	$100
Entertainment (movies, concerts)	$40
Transportation	
Bus fares	$20
Miscellaneous (haircuts, newspapers/magazines, film, etc.)	$30
Clothing	$30
Travel (within Mexico and back to United States to see family)	$200
U.S. taxes	$150
Total Monthly Expenses	**$1,475**
x 12 = Yearly Expenses	$17,700

INCOME PER MONTH

Social Security	$950
Income from investments	$550
Total Monthly Income	**$1,500**
x 12 = Yearly Income	$18,000

French Wine and Ambiance on $34,000 a Year

This couple lives in the French countryside, outside the high-cost areas of Paris or the Côte d'Azur, in a three-bedroom, two-bath house purchased with a mortgage. The couple's budget includes several costly extras: health insurance for their U.S.-based private coverage, as well as a higher than normal postage, telephone, and on-line fees for the Internet, which they use to maintain contact with their children and friends. Due to the higher costs, this couple works part-time to supplement their savings, though they have the consolation of coffee breaks that include French croissants!

EXPENSES PER MONTH

Housing	
Mortgage	$625
Renovations/maintenance	$100
Insurance	$30
Taxes	$30
Utilities	
Electric/gas	$100
Medical	
Health insurance	$330
Life insurance	$245
Doctor/dentist visits	$80
Prescriptions	$30
Communication	
Postage	$20
Phone	$55
Groceries	$240
Dining out	$200
Entertainment (movies, concerts)	$60
Transportation	
Car (used, bought for cash)	$___
Gas/maintenance	$160
Insurance	$ 30
Miscellaneous (haircuts, newspapers/magazines, film, etc.)	$100
Clothing	$100
Travel (overseas and back to States to see family, etc.)	$300
Total Monthly Expenses	**$2,865**
x 12 = Yearly Expenses	$34,380

INCOME PER MONTH

Social Security	$ 1,000
Rental profit on U.S. home	$450
Income from investments	$550
Part-time work	$800
Total Monthly Income	**$2,900**
x 12 = Yearly Income	$34,800

Dining out is cheap here, so are wine and beer. But gasoline is $3.55 a gallon!
—Bob, 65, Albufeira, Portugal

An Algarve Retreat on $26,000 a Year
One couple was fortunate enough to receive an early buyout package from his previous employer, which pays a healthy pension even though he's only in his early fifties. They live quite luxuriously and travel frequently.

However, I found others in Portugal who were very happy and comfortable on much less. The budget below is a compilation of several people I met who were working part-time but still enjoying the beaches and lifestyle.

EXPENSES PER MONTH

Housing	
Mortgage	$575
Renovations/maintenance	$100
Insurance	$30
Taxes	$50
Utilities	
Electric/gas	$50
Medical	
Health insurance	$120
Life insurance	$150
Prescriptions	$20
Communication	
Postage	$20
Phone	$35
Groceries	$175
Meals out	$180
Entertainment (movies, concerts, opera) $35	
Transportation	
Car (used, paid in full)	$–
Gas/maintenance	$120
Car insurance	$50
Miscellaneous (haircuts, newspapers/magazines, film, etc.)	$60
Clothing	$100
Travel	<u>$250</u>
Total Monthly Expenses	**$2,120**
x 12 = Yearly Expenses	$25,440

INCOME PER MONTH

Social Security	$950
Income from investments	$450
Part-time jobs	<u>$750</u>
Total Monthly Income	**$2,150**
x 12 = Yearly Income	$25,800

We found yachting generally less expensive than living in the Northeast U.S.
—Sue and Jim, worldwide cruisers

Worksheet: Your Personal Budget

Once you know your destination and are deeply involved in the planning process you'll be able to estimate specific costs. Be flexible. As you proceed, adjust the figures for better, or worse, or break-even. In our case, for example, we spent less on a used car than we'd planned, but we spend much more on the gas that fills it.

YOUR MONTHLY EXPENSES

Expense	Per Month
Housing	
Rent/mortgage/hotel/boat/camper	_____
Upkeep/repairs	_____
Purchases (furnishing, redecorating)	_____
Taxes (if applicable)	_____
Utilities	
Electricity	_____
Oil/gas	_____
Water	_____
Trash pick-up	_____
Telephone/Internet access	_____
Medical	
Health insurance	_____
Doctor/dentist visits	_____
Prescriptions	_____
Insurance	
Auto	_____
Disability	_____
Apartment/homeowner's	_____
Life	_____
Taxes	
Real estate	_____
Federal	_____
State	_____
Post office/mailing	_____
Groceries	_____
Entertainment/recreation	
Dinners out	_____
Movies/theater/sports events	_____
Hobbies, etc.	_____
Automotive	
Gas/maintenance	_____
Miscellaneous (haircuts, newspapers/magazines, film, etc.)	_____
Language lessons	_____
Clothing	_____
Travel (overseas and back to States to see family, etc.)	_____
Family responsibilities	
Alimony or child support	_____
College or other child costs	_____
Gifts and miscellaneous	_____
Charitable contributions	_____
Total Monthly Expenses	_____
x 12 = Yearly Expenses	_____

Your Monthly Income	Per Month
Investment income	_____
Income from retirement savings (after 59½)	_____
Pension	_____
Social Security	_____
Home rental	_____
Work	_____
Miscellaneous other investments	_____
Total Monthly Income	_____
x 12 = Yearly income	_____

The Bottom Line

Are your expenses and your income close? Then you're in good shape for running away. If the gulf is wide, don't be discouraged. Analyze each figure to see where you can add income or cut expenses to make your adventure possible in a few months or a few years.

We call this genteel poverty!
—Peter, 60, Saint Senoch, France

Tips on Cutting Costs

The next best thing to having more money is needing less. For daily needs, economizing is easier once you're away from the American culture. Sad to say, we Americans love to spend, but overseas the norm tends toward thrift. Most other countries simply don't have the resources of the States, and people take for granted that one must make do, fix things, borrow, and hand down.

Margot in France has mastered the art of *le troc* (barter), which is popular among friends in her rustic *Drôme Provençale* village. Everything is up for exchange, from haircuts to clothes, trucks to computer work.

Another key to managing costs is to carefully consider the things that really give you joy and those expenses that merely result from habit or boredom. Spend on what is vital to you, not to the Joneses. Cut anything extraneous.

Find less expensive alternatives that enable you to enjoy life while saving. Expats living in Guadalajara, Mexico, can spend $7 to see the world-famous Ballet Folklorico, instead of $100 or more on a ticket to a Broadway play.

How you cut costs depends on your own interests, budget, location, and willingness to buckle down. Here are a few other methods suggested by runaways.

Transportation

Become a one- (or zero-) car family. Many runaways survive without the costs of purchase, gas, maintenance, and insurance. They use local transportation, not only more cheaply, but more conveniently. Europeans often live in villages where every service is provided and take a bus or train for excursions.

Many expat couples get by easily without a car, or at the most share one car between them, not the two considered essential in the States.

Rent a car for excursions only. If you want a car for a trip, it's cheaper to rent one for the length of a vacation rather than own a car and maintain it all year simply for two weeks of travel.

If you need a car, buy one used and pay cash. You're not out to impress anyone. You just want to get safely from one charming village to another, so look for a good used car. Pay cash to avoid finance charges and monthly bills. (It also helps keep you on budget when you see the full price of the car all at once.)

We found a sturdy and sporty Citroën with 140,000 kilometers, or approximately 100,000 miles, with all sorts of bells and whistles for the equivalent of $3,500 (my entertainment is the automatic door opener on the key chain). Except for repairing a muffler, service so far has been minimal. Two times we took it to the dealer for minor questions about an oil light and a rear light that didn't work. Both times the dealer fixed the problem free of charge.

> Our three-bedroom, 2½-bath house is in a good area but we waited and waited for a good deal and finally got it for $80,000. Now prices have gone up. But our daily bread is still just 45 cents a loaf.
> —Anne, 61, Albufeira, Portugal

Housing

Down, down, downsize. You're not housing a family and you won't have all your belongings from the States, so rent the smallest furnished apartment or house that you can be comfortable in. The smaller your home is, the less expensive it will be for rent, heating, and other utilities. A small place should require less maintenance too, leaving time for travel and fun.

Buy cheaply and renovate. If you're handy and like puttering around, find a house in need of work and apply sweat equity. If you buy in the right location and use your talents to fix a home up, you could increase its value and even come out with a profit, if you later sell or rent it. Don't count on the latter, however. Remember, purchasing a house incurs up-front costs that must be covered before you benefit from any increase in value. Buying a home is a serious decision and one you should make carefully, knowing that you will most likely stay in a location for a minimum of three years.

Exchange houses. Find a compatible person who wants to live in your area in the States for several months or a year and exchange situations. New Yorkers may be able to exchange with a Parisian who's been transferred temporarily to the U.S. office. Professional services provide names of people wanting to exchange homes (for more information, see chapter 8). You can often set up private arrangements through friends of friends or messages via the Internet. Naturally, you'll check references before getting involved with anyone you don't know. Request a copy of their passport and personal references before even giving out your specific address.

Food

Eat at home. When you live in an area long-term, you can fix most meals yourself, saving dining out for a special restaurant or occasion. This is the biggest cost savings over taking a regular vacation.

Shop local markets for fresh produce. Don't buy imported and prepackaged products. Making meals from fresh products is less expensive, and your adventure will more likely allow you the time to shop for fresh foods. Not only is a pasta primavera with fresh veggies inexpensive, it's healthy.

Eat your main meal at lunch. Restaurants offer full menus at lunch, often the same as what they'd serve at dinner, but less expensive. Eating a large meal earlier is better for your waistline, too, since you can walk off the meal while sightseeing in the afternoon.

Buy the fixed-price menu. Some restaurants, especially in Western European countries such as France, Spain, Ireland, Holland, and Belgium, post the prices outside and include a price for a multicourse meal at a fixed price. These offer a better value than ordering individual items.

Picnic when you travel. Visit local stores and collect fresh bread, meats or cheeses, fruit, and that tempting pastry. Then find a glorious spot to have your picnic. You'll spend less money and eat better than when you pay inflated autoroute, train, or ferry prices.

Health Care

Use the local medical system. Though known for its advanced medical care, the U.S. medical system is among the costliest in the world. Many countries have equal or even better services far less expensively. Ask other expats or locals which doctors they recommend. You may be pleasantly surprised when you pay $20 for a doctor's visit that would be $75 in the States. Some countries, such as Mexico, even allow expats access to that country's low-cost insurance plans once they've become residents.

Take care of yourself. Prevention offers the best opportunity to cut medical costs. Don't overdo food, drink, exercise, or sun overseas. When you feel tired or think a cold's coming on, take that nap. After all, you're here to relax, so take advantage of it.

Lifestyle
Use coupons and discounts. Watch for the discounts provided overseas on trains, buses, movies, museum passes, and the like. Seniors often get special savings, but you don't always have to be over sixty-five. Sometimes being sixty or even fifty-five suffices. Reductions sometimes exist for transportation, for example, when two people travel together or travel during certain off-peak times.

Organizations such as Entertainment Publications offer discount coupon books with reduced prices on hotels, restaurants, and services on leisure activities such as museums, boat rides, and theaters. Entertainment Publications offers books for several locations overseas, mostly for cities such as Paris and London. The easiest way to find out what's available overseas is to call Entertainment Publications's toll-free number at (800) 445-4137. They'll tell you if there's an Entertainment book covering your destination. Incidentally, overseas editions may be in another language (the Paris edition is in French), so if that will be a problem, ask before you order.

Cut out all that paper. Use old dishrags to clean with, not expensive paper towels. Keep the plastic bags you get at stores to use for storage and to line small wastebaskets. Save decorative papers from gifts; reuse them for your own gift giving.

Make it, reuse it, or make do. Many of the things you need, you already have: clothes, for example. I discovered that I have more of them than would ever fit in an overseas closet.

Don't let money hold you back. Be creative with your plans, finding less expensive ways to fund your adventure. Sell unneeded belongings. Save diligently. Your adventure can be affordable. Some adventures—like the Peace Corps—even pay you!

> *The price of doctors here—everything, in fact—is negotiable and based on personal relationship. All jobs are done by knowing somebody. I have a dentist who won't let me pay him. I offer but he says, "No, you're my friend." He knows I'll help him out whenever I can too. The economy often functions like this, without money.*
> —Judy, 62, Athens, Greece

6

The Work Option

EVERYTHING THAT IS REALLY GREAT
AND INSPIRING IS CREATED BY THE INDIVIDUAL
WHO CAN LABOR IN FREEDOM.
—Albert Einstein

You may be running away from work as you knew it, but finding some meaningful work to do overseas part-time, or even full-time if you so desire, can put extra vigor into your life. It enables you to meet people—usually it's a built-in requirement—and puts extra cash in your pocket, enabling you to enjoy other new interests or extra travel.

I should also note that working overseas isn't nearly as onerous when you consider the long holidays enjoyed in most countries outside the United States. Six weeks a year is common in Europe, for example, with many holidays creating four-day weekends. Even if you have a job overseas, you'll have more time to enjoy travel, hobbies, and social occasions.

I asked one expat in Switzerland how he managed to work, teach, and volunteer for American Citizens Abroad. His immediate comment said it all: "Remember, I'm not still dealing with two-week vacations, like in the States."

CAN YOU WORK AS A FOREIGNER?

Before you can find work overseas you must first have the right to work. Naturally, countries want to keep jobs for their nationals and legal residents. This can prevent you from taking a formal job in many countries.

However, you can work for a United States firm that provides the proper paperwork for a work visa, or a foreign firm requiring a specific set of services that cannot be found in their nationals (for example, knowledge of a computer program none of their people can handle).

What you can do depends on the country. In countries with high unemployment, such as France or Germany, you'll have difficulty finding legal work. Others are more lax about enforcing the work laws. Or, you can simply work for yourself, supplying a service or handicraft. In Portugal, Bob uses his admirable skills as a master furniture restorer to refinish antiques for many affluent Brits who are moving to the Algarve. Right now he has more work than he wants in retirement.

Irish or Italian? You May Be Eligible for an EU Passport

Why would you want a European Union passport? Strictly because, with one, you're able to work legally in any European Union country, which vastly enlarges your opportunities, not only to work but to live anywhere you please in the EU without the hassles of long-term visas and such.

Some people are eligible for an EU passport and don't realize it. If your grandfather was born in Ireland and you can prove it via birth records, you can apply for an Irish passport based on your heritage. Since Ireland is part of the European Union, your Irish passport, which you can have without losing your American citizenship, enables you to travel and work throughout the European Union. I missed this by one generation. Sigh . . .

Other countries, such as Italy, have a similar policy on ancestry, so give your family history a close look.

> *The easiest ways into working in Europe seem to be through a technical specialty, e.g., computers. Some people get dual nationality or working status through ancestry.*
> —Doug, 43, Basel, Switzerland

FINDING JOBS OVERSEAS

If you must work overseas, then find a job before you leave the States. If you insist on leaving without a job, at least investigate the opportunities for your destination thoroughly and develop marketable skills so you're fully prepared to find work once you're there.

Depending on your current skills, the country where you'll be living, and the amount of money you'll need to survive, you could have countless possibilities for jobs. If you're in a position to arrange with your company to transfer you overseas, you can begin your adventure under the corporate umbrella.

Many of us simply want the cross-cultural or travel experience. In that case, the work you choose could be temporary, providing some extras that keep you from spending your retirement stash.

Full-time or part-time work can be an integral part of your immersion into the local culture. Here are some possible ways to earn money overseas.

International Companies

You'll see familiar logos all over the world, ranging from Coca-Cola to IBM, AT&T to Texas Instruments, and more smaller companies than you'd ever imagine. These companies staff their overseas offices with nationals of the country as well as specialists they bring from the States. If you already work for a company with international ties, ask the personnel department where you work or your boss about opportunities for transfer overseas.

Read classified ads in your local paper and international papers such as the *International Herald Tribune.* Just before leaving for France I saw an ad in the *Atlanta Journal*, of all places, which suited my qualifications, for an advertising copywriter in Brussels. We had already made our plans in France, but it was tempting.

Start learning the language of your destination. It's your ace. Even if you're looking for a job with a U.S. firm overseas, you'll need to work in the local culture, and knowing the language will give you a distinct advantage.

Short-Term Jobs

Temps through professional agencies overseas usually need a visa that permits working in that country. You stand a better chance of finding menial jobs, which are in high supply but of little interest to the local labor force. Menial jobs are easily filled by transients, and the local authorities often ignore the rules when the grapes need picking or the resorts need more waiters who speak English—especially in popular tourist spots.

Look for job openings available for English speakers at tourist resorts or tour companies. Check local bulletin boards like those found in grocery stores, lodgings such as youth hostels (which, despite their name, house travelers of any age), and English-language bookstores. Check the classifieds in your destination newspapers.

One enterprising woman we met in a restaurant in the Algarve had sent her resume to a list of prestigious Relais et Châteaux hotels found throughout the world. She ended up with two offers, one in Portugal and the other in Switzerland. When she tired of the Algarve, she planned to move on.

> *One of the first people I talked to upon my arrival here was*
> *a 70ish American lawyer who had been here for some 35 years and*
> *advised me to cobble together whatever work I could and not wait for that*
> *one big, fat-paying job. It was great advice, which I took to heart and*
> *allowed me to ultimately succeed—or at least be able to stay here.*
>
> —Edward, 38, Geneva, Switzerland

Teaching English

If you're serious about teaching English, you can take a TESL (Teaching English as a Second Language) course. The certificate provides credentials and makes you more acceptable to the higher-level schools and institutes. A certificate is necessary for the truly professional person who intends to work full-time as a teacher. Courses are offered through some universities. Call locally or check the ads in *Transitions Abroad* magazine or other international publications.

If you merely want to supplement your income with some part-time teaching here and there, taking a formal TESL course may be overkill. It will be costly, require several months, and if you don't live in a location where TESL is offered, you'll have to travel to take it.

One solution is to get training locally and less expensively through volunteer service. Volunteer to teach English in the United States for a year or more before your departure. Literacy Volunteers of America, for one, provides training for free, though they require you to purchase the materials, which cost approximately $35. The materials are then yours to take with you overseas, and they form a good basis for lesson plans. Having the course provides you with the confidence to go out and find students.

English schools are prevalent in the Far East, especially in Japan. English teachers are used for company employees, in schools, and for individual tutoring. U.S. English is preferred in many areas of the Far East, though British English is often preferred in Europe and Hong Kong.

The YMCA has a program whereby retired people can assist the national council in Taiwan as teachers of English as a second language. For more information, contact OSCY Program Administration, YMCA of the USA, International Division, 101 N. Wacker Dr., Chicago, IL 60606; telephone (800) 872-9622; fax (312) 977-0884.

If you're already a teacher in the States, check for teacher exchange programs, or apply for jobs overseas in international or military schools. Some contacts include: International School Services, 15 Rozel Road, PO Box 5910, Princeton, NJ 08543; telephone (609) 452-0990. The Department of Defense, Office of Dependents Schools, Teacher Recruitment, Room 112 Hoffman Bldg. No.1, 2461 Eisenhower Avenue, Alexandria, VA 22331-1100; telephone (202) 325-0885.

> *When he retired at age 55, Dave decided to see if he could teach science overseas. He went to a hiring conference in New York City and was hired to teach science at Colegio Internacional de Caracas . . . and the director of CIC hired me to be his secretary. Our daughter, Susan, was just graduating from teacher's college, and he hired her to teach third grade!*
> —Susan, 65, Caracas, Venezuela

English Consulting
Publishers and publicity houses need English speakers to edit books, brochures, and newsletters, usually in technical fields, such as computer science. You'll need to know the local language, though it works better if you work in a team with someone who knows the idioms in the language and can translate it roughly, while you polish it into good English.

> *We came with a retirement mind-set, but when costs rose,*
> *we began working part-time. But though we're both working, we're*
> *here, happy to be living abroad and having a great time. I don't want*
> *to be on my deathbed and regret not doing what I wanted.*
> —Bob, 69, Albufeira, Portugal

Arts and Crafts
If you've got the skills to restore antiques, make puppets, knit, crochet, do hand-tinted photographs, or draw portraits of people or views of popular tourist sites, you may be able to sell your products locally at a fair, market, or through word of mouth.

Bob and Anne fell in love with the Algarve and moved there permanently seven years ago. However, the place had become more popular than when they first moved there and prices rose, so they went through their retirement funds faster than planned. Now they're working in part-time jobs they enjoy, Anne at a local radio station and Bob restoring antiques. As he says, "I'm in paradise here, and I'm doing work I enjoy. It beats having to return."

Resorts
Resorts around the world need personnel, and in areas where the guests tend to be English speakers, hotels and restaurants look for people who can interact with these visitors (of course, knowing the local language is helpful, too).

I've even heard that Club Med, known previously as the haunt of the youthful, is accepting energetic older workers. Club Med is found throughout the world, in some of the most beautiful locales, including beaches, mountains, and cities. See their Web site at www.clubmed.com for job information.

Entrepreneurship
Some people don't view their running away experience as a chance to kick back, but instead have sought out new challenges. If your idea of fun is to uncover and expand a new market overseas, then there are countless opportunities in developing countries, though they're far beyond the scope of this book. Groups involved in international marketing will provide more input and real-world advice.

Remember that you don't have to join the rat race again to work for yourself. One talented expat in France's Loire Valley was a technical artist in his "first" life. He brought his Mac with him and, besides its being handy for printing invitations to his garden parties, he's putting it to productive use by studying graphic programs with an eye towards designing Web sites for businesses.

> *I was with the foreign service here, but what attracted me to go*
> *out on my own and work here (aside from being partially insane) was the*
> *challenge of bringing computer connectivity to a virgin market. Now, of course,*
> *that market has grown to encompass all of Africa and the Middle East!*
> —Jim, 51, Rabat, Morocco

ARE YOU CUT OUT TO WORK OVERSEAS?

• Do you have a transferable skill?

• Do you speak the local language well enough to manage on the job?

• Are you willing to adjust to different cultural standards at work, such as different attitudes toward punctuality, meetings, deference toward supervisors?

• Can your ego stand a menial job if that's all that's available?

OTHER SOURCES FOR WORK OVERSEAS

If you want a formal job overseas, be persistent. Use all your resources and networking skills. Read classifieds in local papers, but especially those in international papers, such as the *International Herald Tribune* or your destination's daily newspaper. Check help-wanted ads in journals relevant to your field, to see if there's a need for representation overseas. Research job opportunities through specialty publications you can find in libraries and bookstores. Here are a few that might prove helpful:

Institute of International Education (IIE), 809 UN Plaza, New York, NY 10017, (212) 984-5413. IIE offers reference books, foreign university catalogs, study-abroad brochures, and other materials that can be consulted by students and nonstudents. The book *Teaching Abroad* lists employment and study opportunities overseas for U.S. teachers.

For a current list of IIE publications, with prices and ordering information, write to the IIE Publications Service at the above address. Books can be purchased by mail or in person. General information on IIE programs and services is available from regional offices in Atlanta, Chicago, Denver, Houston, San Francisco, and Washington, D.C.

International Employment Hotline, Box 3030, Oakton, VA 22124. $39 year for this monthly newsletter.

International Jobs: Where They Are and How to Get Them, by Eric Kocher, Addison-Wesley Publishing Company.

Teaching English Abroad: Talk Your Way Around the World!, by Susan Griffith, distributed by Peterson's Guides.

Taxing Results

Before taking a job overseas, consider that it will embroil you in the tax structure of the country involved. In some cases, due to the more highly socialized nature of the countries, these taxes will be considerably more than you, as a U.S. citizen, are accustomed to. For a minor job, you may not want to become enmeshed in the bureaucracy.

However, one IRS rule does provide a tax benefit. You may be able to exclude up to $70,000 of your foreign earned income. This exclusion applies to both spouses, if you both work overseas, for a total of $140,000 in exclusions. You may even have an employer-provided housing allowance excluded from income. Of course, you still may have to pay taxes to the country where you're working. This all depends on the job and whether you're working for a U.S. or foreign firm. If you're considering a job overseas, talk to your tax advisor to see how it will affect your financial position.

Returning to Work in the States

If you decide to return to the United States and a job, will you be able to? This depends on your credentials, maintaining your skills overseas, and presenting your time off as a benefit to future employers.

If you have a good job and are able to take a leave of absence or sabbatical, your job will be waiting when you return. If you're leaving your job and think it's even remotely possible that you'll want to return to work, lay the groundwork before you leave. Maintain a network of contacts in the States while you're gone. Stay current with news and skills necessary in your field. And accent the positive.

Your time off has made you more marketable rather than less. You've increased your confidence, learned new skills, and you have one ace in the hole—your experience has given you a mystique that sets you apart from the pack. You may get a foot in the door for an interview just because some restless personnel director wants to know more about your adventure.

A history of good jobs prior to your sabbatical shows your ability and will encourage someone to believe you really are good at what you do. One long-term sabbatical after years of work does not show instability, as long as you explain the time away and do not look like someone who will keep taking sabbaticals.

Your chances of finding a job when you return improve if you have a special skill, for example, in computers, finance, or marketing. But, be realistic. If you're at midlife now, you'll be older when you return. So if work is a necessity, determine your chances of returning to find it. My feeling is that, if you're the type of person who had the spirit to go on an adventure overseas, you're the type who's flexible enough to find employment when you return. It just may not be the same fast-track job you might have worked your way up to before leaving. But would you really want that again?

Tips to Tackle Returning Interviews
Here are tips for maneuvering yourself back into the job market if you return to work in the States:
• Stay current in your field. Information, equipment, and systems change. Read trade journals and stay up on what's happening while you're gone.
• Be prepared to take a refresher course when you return, if necessary.
• Use your international experience. Marketers, accounting firms, telecommunication companies, pharmaceutical companies, newspapers and magazines, schools, and certainly, the travel industry, all have international ties. Emphasize your newfound skills in language and cultural relations.
• Explain your experience honestly, emphasizing your new abilities based on the travel. You may have learned a new language and have an international perspective, all of which can make you more marketable.
• Focus your resume on what you've done rather than on a strictly chronological order.
• Use your adventure to set you apart from the crowd. Who wouldn't prefer spicing up their workday by interviewing you instead of any of a hundred other applicants, if only to find out how you did it or more about Italy for their vacation.
• Be prepared to explain your adventure in business terms. Explain why you took the time off and what you accomplished or learned that would benefit your prospective employer and why you want to begin working again. Avoid personal adventures. Don't say, "Hey, the wine was great and I went to the beach all day." You might instead say that you wanted to learn about other cultures (yeah, wine culture) and studied the local flora and fauna (the girls were topless at Saint-Tropez).
• Whatever you do, don't be defensive about your time away. Respond positively.

Thinking of your experiences in a positive light may give you the confidence to look for a good job and find it on your return. But, the fact is, you may not want to return to a steady job after life overseas. It's difficult returning to the rigorous hours and short vacations that are common in the United States when you've lived in cultures where two-hour lunches and six weeks' vacation are the norm.

Be flexible. You may discover better work overseas, even if it's, like Bob, refinishing antiques, or like me, writing about it.

7

Making the Most of
Your Time Away

TO KNOW HOW TO FREE ONESELF
IS NOTHING; THE ARDUOUS THING IS TO KNOW
WHAT TO DO WITH ONE'S FREEDOM.

—André Gide

The most successful runaways are those who begin by planning what they want to achieve. Achieve? Did I dare use that goal-oriented word for what should be a thrilling time of freedom and adventure?

Yes, because you now have a fabulous opportunity to follow your dream, but you must determine the goal and set a course for it.

PLAN FOR PLEASURE, NOT BOREDOM

People who have put heart and soul into working or raising children for most of their adult years often don't know what to do with a sudden increase of free time. You'll need to do a little soul-searching *before* you leave that safe job haven and the routine of your present life to venture into that big twenty-four-hour world of unstructured hours. Having interests will help you avoid a problem that occurs when people head overseas without a clear plan—what one friend who moved to Portugal described as "bored expats spending their time in the local bar for lack of anything better to do."

Actually, this particular woman and her husband know well how to benefit from the gift of time. They stored up a number of small goals they wanted to achieve long before they packed up the moving van. They had an abiding interest in archaeology, so they signed on with a group that makes periodic forays to different sites throughout Portugal and nearby Spain. Opera is another love, so they stocked up on CDs before coming to Portugal and make visits to Seville, an hour-and-a-half drive, for special performances. Never having had the leisure in their work lives for games and such, they decided to learn bridge. Plus, they're discovering the fresh local produce and trying new recipes.

None of these activities is particularly grandiose; nevertheless, this couple had a specific set of interests that they were ready to follow up on—when they're not sunning by their pool overlooking the Algarve coast.

So start a list for yourself. What is it you've always wanted to do? Write that novel? Learn photography? Skipper a sailboat in the Caribbean? Hike Germany's lush Black Forest trails? Jot down the things you want to do that are specific to your destination, plus things you've always wanted to do but never had time for before running away.

Don't worry if the list is long; prioritize it to break it down to manageable chunks. Then you'll have a reminder of things you wanted to do on the mornings when you wake up with the sun and feel at loose ends, wondering what you will do other than sleep or eat or drink wine. Better to have more things than you can possibly accomplish than too little.

Living overseas is a learning experience in itself. In addition, a myriad of formal and informal programs can be explored, providing opportunities to expand your mind and add new interests to your life.

If you have a specific interest you'd like to explore—let's say photography or antiques or history—you may enjoy a formal study abroad program. A formal program, rather than independent study, may also give you more confidence on your first foray overseas. For the single traveler, a formal program provides the opportunity to meet like-minded people overseas and share the learning experiences within a group setting.

Specialized programs combine learning with overseas travel opportunities for adults. Such programs are short-term for the most part, but they offer interesting diversions outside the realm of a normal vacation and may be part of your runaway plan. The options range from casual and inexpensive programs to more formal, even elite, diploma or certificate programs for the professional or serious amateur. You'll find examples of some of these below. For additional activities and programs, check advertising in various publications devoted to overseas living, such as *International Living*, the *International Herald Tribune*, or books devoted to study abroad programs. Or contact universities directly to see if they're affiliated with schools overseas that offer study programs for adults.

So get those brain cells churning and consider the possibilities. Being prepared with enjoyable projects will keep your mind active and your spirits elevated. That's the key to making a successful transition overseas.

ACTIVITIES THAT TRAVEL WELL

Learn a Language

As I've said before, make an effort to learn the language of the country you'll be living in—or even one you'd just like to visit. Living in another country is a wonderful opportunity to practice a new language. It's a joy to be able to communicate, even a little. Your world will expand exponentially with each new word because you'll understand aspects of the people and culture beyond the usual tourist sights. Besides, recent studies have shown that learning a new language actually expands the brain's capacity. Not a bad idea as we reach middle age.

> *If you can get out of the U. S. and live in a foreign country, do it.*
> *There's a lot to learn, interesting people, and situations to experience*
> *and opportunities to enrich your own and others' lives.*
> —Frank, 53, Bangkok, Thailand

Public and private universities, adult education courses, and specialty language schools offer an array of classes that enable you to begin learning a language. Libraries and bookstores offer books, tapes, and videos to improve grammar, vocabulary, and comprehension. And, for the ultimate experience, many educational groups offer overseas programs that enable adult learners to immerse themselves wholeheartedly in a language by living and learning in a country where it's used.

It would be impossible to list the countless programs available, but here are some of the more famous options.

Alliance Française. One of the great European language schools, Alliance Française is based in Paris but operates French language schools in more than 130 countries, including major cities throughout the United States. Classes are ongoing, with levels from beginner to advanced. They meet for ten to twelve weeks each session, or you can take private classes. For information, in the United States: Alliance Française, 2142 Wyoming Avenue NW, Washington, DC 20008; telephone (202) 234-7911. In France: Alliance Française de Paris, Boulevard Raspail 101, 75270 Paris CEDEX 06, France.

Instituto Allende. Begun by an American decades ago, the Instituto has grown to become one of the most famous Spanish language training schools in the world. It's located in the charming town of San Miguel de Allende, known for its artistic community. For information: Instituto Allende, Ancha de San Antonia #20, San Miguel de Allende, Gto, Mexico; telephone 011-52 415-2-01-90; fax 011-52-415-2-45-38; e-mail: ktarana@mpsnet.com.mx; Web site: www.instituto-allende.edu.mx/reg.htm.

Goethe-Institut. The Institut offers German language training, a library of German language books, and presents Germanic cultural events. You'll find regional offices in major cities in the United States and Canada. For information: Goethe-Institut, 1014 Fifth Avenue, New York, NY 10028; telephone (212) 439-8700. Or you may find a regional office in major cities. Web site: www.goethe.de.

Inlingua. Inlingua has over 300 language training centers in cities around the world, including the United States, Europe, Latin America, Japan, and Korea. Based in Bern, Switzerland, Inlingua also offers cross-cultural training, translation, and interpretation services. For information: telephone (800) INLINGUA.

Berlitz. Berlitz has over 330 locations worldwide for language training, and according to Berlitz, they'll provide training in any spoken language in the world. Methods include private and group instruction. Berlitz also offers cross-cultural awareness training, interpretation, translation, and study abroad programs. For information: telephone (800) 457-7958; Web site: www.berlitz.com.

Plan Theme Tours
Taking a trip may sound superfluous, since this is the point of your overall adventure. However, keep in mind that, even if you settle in one area overseas, it's easier to plan day trips within the country and to other countries— trips that in the United States would simply get you to another state.

Develop interests and plan day trips around them. If you settle in the Tuscany hill country of Italy and enjoy cooking, plan an overnight to Bologna to try the original—and supposedly world's best—spaghetti sauce. Then try to duplicate it at home.

If you collect pottery in Mexico, plan short trips to local markets or specialized workshops. Study the various styles and techniques. Or, learn to make your own pots by signing up for lessons and trying the techniques you've discovered.

Discover Your Roots
If you'll be near areas where your family originated, research your family tree. It's interesting to explore old records and grave sites for the names of a long-lost ancestor.

Start before you leave the States by gathering all the information you can from family members, including relevant birth dates and ancestral places overseas. Books, computer software, and genealogical groups on the Internet provide research help. The Church of Latter Day Saints offers comprehensive genealogical information, including research tips and a massive library of contacts and records. (No, you don't have to be a Mormon to take advantage of the services.) Once you're overseas, you can check specific church or city hall records and follow any other fascinating leads you uncover.

Get Fit

Use your new lifestyle to put more life in your body. Spend spare time walking interesting village streets, hiking through vineyards, riding a bike along a tranquil river path, swimming, or playing tennis. Participate with groups to make new friends, or take a class to learn a new sports skill. All this exercise has a wonderful side benefit: it helps burn off the tempting new foods you'll try.

To find groups active in your sport, ask at the town hall where you're living, watch for posters on planned events, and buy the community paper. The latter almost always lists neighborhood activities, the time and location of the events, and contact numbers.

Develop Your Artistic Self

Paint, write, sculpt, or learn photography. Even if you've never thought of yourself as artistic, you can enjoy the process, and no one has to see the results if you don't care to share. Perhaps you'll even discover a latent talent. Take classes and make friends at the same time. Most places you'll want to visit have native crafts, as well as the fine arts.

Mexico's *Instituto Allende* is located in a sixteenth-century colonial town so pretty it's been declared a Mexican national monument. The courses offered include oil painting, watercolor, and sculpture, while the surrounding streets are filled with artists, art galleries, and inspiration. (The Instituto is also known for its language classes.) For information: Instituto Allende, Ancha de San Antonia #20, San Miguel de Allende, Gto, Mexico; telephone 011-52 415-2-01-90; fax 011-52-415-2-45-38; e-mail: ktarana@mpsnet.com.mx; Web site: www.instituto-allende.edu.mx/reg.htm.

For other areas check the ads in recent art magazines; they're usually jammed with trips that combine classes with visits overseas. Or ask at local art associations if they have any upcoming trips that are open to fellow artists in the community.

You can also join local art classes abroad. You'll benefit twice, by expressing yourself and becoming involved in the community.

> *We compiled a network book for other English speakers here, with names of doctors, lawyers, schools—all the info we could think of to make the move here easier. It was a miracle of a thing.*
> —Judy, 62, Athens, Greece

Cook a New Cuisine

Part of the joy of traveling is discovering new tastes in food and drink. Don't settle for just eating though; try making some recipes yourself. Markets in old-world countries are fascinating places, filled with fresh-from-the-next-field vegetables and fruits, plus interesting cheeses, meats, and fishes. Explore the market; then go back to your kitchen and create your own specialties. Even those of us who didn't like cooking after putting in a full day at work in the States are discovering that cooking overseas is fun.

If you're serious about learning new skills, you can sign up for overseas classes. Find them locally. Or, if money is no object, you may want to splurge on one of these prestigious schools overseas:

Le Cordon Bleu. Long renowned, Le Cordon Bleu schools excel in the culinary arts. Master chefs train students from around the globe; diploma courses are available for professionals, though serious amateurs can start with certificate courses. The original began in Paris, but schools are also available in London, Sydney, Ottawa, and Tokyo. For information, U.S. Corporate Office: (800) 457-CHEF. Paris: Le Cordon Bleu, 8, rue Léon Delhomme, 75015 Paris, France; telephone 33 (0)1 53 68 22 50; fax 33 (0)1 48 56 03 96. London: Le Cordon Bleu, 114 Marylebone Lane, London, WIM 6HH, Great Britain; telephone 44/0 171 935 3503; fax 44/0 171 935 7621. Ottawa: Le Cordon Bleu, 400-1390 Prince of Wales Dr., Ottawa, Ontario K2C 3N6; telephone (613) 224-8603; fax (613) 224-9966; e-mail: macinnis@lcbottawa.com. Sydney: Le Cordon Bleu, 250 Blaxland Road, Ryde, Sydney NSW 2112; telephone 61/2 808 8307; fax 61/2 809 3346. Tokyo: Le Cordon Bleu, ROOB-1 28-113, Saragaku-Cho, Daikanyama, Shibuya-ku, Tokyo 150; telephone 81/3 5489 0141; fax 81/3 5489 0145. Overall Web Site: www.cordonbleu.net/textsite/school.htm.

At Home with Patricia Wells: Cooking in Provence. An American in Paris, Patricia Wells is the *International Herald Tribune*'s restaurant critic and author of several popular books on French cooking and bistros. She offers exclusive four- or five-day cooking programs at her eighteenth-century home in Provence, with visits to markets, vineyards, shops, and local restaurants. For information: Judith Jones, 708 Sandown Place, Raleigh, NC 27615; fax (919) 846-2081; e-mail: jj708@mindspring.com.

Create New Space

If you're permanently settled somewhere overseas, warm up your surroundings with flowers from the garden or local arts and crafts for your living room. In France, one group of expats visits the village *brocantes* (antique markets) every chance they get. They browse up and down the tables, occasionally finding a treasure to add to their home overseas or to a collection. Another has transformed his yard by collecting a wide range of flowering plants that his guests enjoy admiring and learning about.

Discover the Great Outdoors

Revel in the scenery as you explore a new area's flora and fauna. From Costa Rica's rain forest to Swiss mountain peaks, you can get serious about archaeology, geology, bird watching, fly fishing, collecting butterflies, or capturing memories with your camera. A few groups that offer adult programs include:

Archaeological Institute of America. A nonprofit cultural and educational organization chartered by the U.S. Congress, this is the oldest and largest archaeological organization in North America. The group conducts fieldwork in Africa, Asia, Europe, and North and South America and presents tours of archaeological interest from the prehistoric caves of France to sailing the Nile and more.

They generate a variety of archaeological publications including *The Archaeological Fieldwork Opportunities Bulletin,* which is put out on January 1 each year, listing over 300 opportunities for volunteers to participate in field sites worldwide. The *Bulletin* costs approximately $11 plus $4 postage. For the *Bulletin,* contact Kendall-Hunt Publishing at (800) 228-0810. For information: Archaeological Institute of America, 656 Beacon Street, Boston, MA 02215-2010; telephone (617) 353-9361; fax (617) 353-6550; e-mail: aia@bu.edu.

Earthwatch. This international nonprofit organization supports scientific field research through volunteers who work with scientists on projects worldwide. Fees range from $650 to $1,995 or more for food, housing, and transportation, not including airfare. For information: Earthwatch, 680 Mount Auburn St., Watertown, MA 02272; telephone (800) 776-0188; fax (617) 926-8532; e-mail: info@earthwatch.org; Web site: www.earthwatch.org.

National Geographic Society—On Tour. Trips last ten days to three weeks, with an average cost of $3,500. While these are travel tours, they differ slightly from the usual in that the Society offers trips to China, which are difficult to find, as well as other destinations. For information: National Geographic Society—On Tour, 1000 16th St. NW, Suite 350, Washington, DC 20036-5705; telephone (888) 966-8687.

Smithsonian Institution. Study tours take adults primarily to Europe for ten days to two weeks, with prices from $3,000 to $7,000. For information: Smithsonian Study Tours and Seminars, 1100 Jefferson Dr., SW (MRC 702), Room 3077, Washington, DC 20560; telephone (202) 357-4700; fax (202) 633-9250.

*We are both avid archaeology buffs, so we joined the local group here and
go along on their trips to sites throughout Spain and Portugal . . . and sometimes
beyond. It's a wonderful opportunity to expand our knowledge of the area.*
—Claire, 45, Algarve, Portugal

Become a Bookworm

A sunny beach will be ideal for catching up on your reading—as will a cozy
cabin with a fireplace, when it's raining. Yes, it will rain on your adventure,
so make a list of all the good books you've been wanting to read and pack
up a bunch of them to take with you overseas. After you've read them, trade
around to create an informal lending library with other English speakers
wherever you may be.

By the way, don't panic if you run out of English-language books. Most
large cities abroad have a bookstore especially dedicated to them (in Paris,
there are at least three English bookstores I know of), or a large local bookstore may have an English-language section. I've found English-language
paperbacks at French antique fairs, and a French friend whose deceased
husband spoke English gave us three cartons of them.

If you have a computer, you can select from classics to the most recent
best-sellers, from biographies to travel guides and more, via online bookstores. For starters, see Amazon (www.amazon.com) or Barnes and Noble
(www.barnesandnoble.com).

Take Up a Topic

Choose a subject you've always wanted to know more about. Are you interested in the history of World War II? Vegetable gardening? A famous artist
you've always admired? Direct your reading toward becoming an expert on
the subject. Take classes and join special-interest groups.

Some groups are specially designed for adult learners, offering a wide
sampling of programs to explore.

Elderhostel. For people fifty-five or older, the nonprofit Elderhostel organization presents a variety of programs ranging from music to literature, history,
the arts, geology, folk life, plants, biking, computers, and more, in the United
States, Canada, and over seventy countries overseas, including Italy, Great
Britain, Bermuda, Denmark, Finland, France, Holland, Norway, Sweden,
Germany, and Israel. Elderhostel is inexpensive, since participants stay in
school dorms or other reasonably priced locations. The programs have no
special requirements for previous degrees or diplomas, just the simple desire
to participate and enjoy the opportunity for personal enrichment. The group
puts out a series of catalogs for their United States, Canadian, and international programs. If requesting information, be sure to specify which location

you're interested in. For information, contact Elderhostel, 75 Federal St., Boston, MA 02110-1941; Web site: www.elderhostel.org.

TraveLearn. Adults from thirty to eighty can participate in learning vacations through more than 300 universities. Programs include lectures, seminars, and hands-on field experiences, but without exams, grades, or attendance requirements. Groups are small, the average being fourteen people, but no more than twenty. First-class accommodations are available for couples or singles. For information: TraveLearn, PO Box 315, Lakeville, PA 18438; telephone: (800) 235-9114; Web site: www.travelearn.com.

Center for Global Education at Augsburg College. These educational travel programs of one to three weeks can be integrated into a longer sabbatical for adults wanting to study Latin America, southern Africa, the Caribbean, the Middle East, or the Asia/Pacific region. For information: Center for Global Education, 2211 Riverside Avenue, Box 307, Minneapolis, MN 55454; telephone (800) 299-8889; e-mail: globaled@augsburg.edu; Web site: www.augsburg.edu/global.

Make New Friends

Whatever you choose to do, don't sit on the sidelines. Participate and meet new people, whether English-speaking or native to your chosen locale. Trade language lessons with someone, helping them learn English in exchange for lessons in their language. Invite them for a drink or a lunch and enjoy learning more about their lives.

Expatriate groups thrive in most major cities overseas, so ask at the embassy or consulate, or review a local English-language newspaper for information.

> *Vacations are but teasers. Living and working in a*
> *place gives one the opportunity to really savor the flavor.*
> —Anne, 61, Albufeira, Portugal

Volunteer

After years of earning a living, you now have the time to give back. Volunteering is one way to share your knowledge and abilities. You, in turn, will benefit from the joy of helping others as you make new friends in the community. You can participate as a volunteer on an informal or formal basis. If you're interested in a specialized program, consider one of the following:

The Peace Corps. Got a yen to travel, no cash, and a desire to serve your fellow man? The Peace Corps is not just for kids; it places adult volunteers in ninety-four countries around the world. They work in a variety of fields, with all living, travel, and medical expenses covered during the length of service, which includes three months' training and about twenty-seven months on the job. Amazingly enough, the Peace Corps has no upper age limit. Married couples can serve, though you must both apply and be accepted by the Peace Corps. Most assignments require a bachelor's degree, some require a master's degree, and some may require several years of work experience instead of, or in addition to, your bachelor's degree.

You must apply at least six to eight months prior to the time you're available to leave. For information or an application: telephone (800) 424-8580; Web site: www.peacecorps.gov/.

> *I had already been to Pakistan with the foreign service and when*
> *I got back to the States it wasn't nearly as exciting, so I volunteered for*
> *the Peace Corps. It was an adventure and you get the feel of the places and*
> *the people. I worked as a secretary with a medical team in Africa.*
> *I met my husband there and later we moved here.*
> —Mary, 61, Moncarpacho, Portugal

Volunteers for Peace. This nonprofit organization coordinates international work camps to assist community development and international education. An inexpensive way to live and work, most two- to three-week programs cost just $175, including room and board. (You can sign up for more than one program.) This is a working experience. VFP does not recommend its programs for tourism or a cheap vacation. VFP puts out an *International Workcamp Directory* that lists more than 800 programs in over sixty-five countries ($12 U.S. postage paid). For information: VFP, 43 Tiffany Rd., Belmont, VT 05730; telephone (802) 259-2759; fax (802) 259-2922; e-mail: vfp@vfp.org; Web site: www.vfp.org.

WorldTeach. An international social service program, WorldTeach places volunteers as teachers in developing countries that request assistance. No formal teaching is required, though programs do require a bachelor's degree (B.A./B.S.). These volunteer positions pay a modest stipend for the academic year in which you participate, but you pay a fee, currently $4,400 to cover airfare, administration, health insurance, and lodging. For information: WorldTeach, Harvard Institute for International Development, One Eliot St., Cambridge, MA 20138-5705; telephone (617) 495-5527; fax (617) 495-1599; e-mail: Info@worldteach.org; Web site: www.igc.org/worldteach.

> *I do, and have done, workshops with schools and ag colleges . . . on how to*
> *grow everything needed to feed a family of seven on one hectare of land and have*
> *money to spare. The program was very successful in Latin America.*
> —Rulon, 71, Mexico

8

Finding a Home Overseas

LEARN A NEW LANGUAGE
AND GET A NEW SOUL.
—Czech proverb

Once you've determined the general destination for your adventure, you'll need to find that specific place to call home. It can be an apartment in a bustling city or a motor home on the open road, a tranquil farm or a house in a village. Your final decision will hinge on the location itself, the size and amenities you require, your budget, and the specific accommodations available at the time of your adventure.

Quite possibly your final choice may result from a touch of whimsy. Let it happen. Several people didn't find their homes until the last minute. Peter and Dana looked for a home on each vacation for seven years until they found their dream property. Bob and Anne rented for almost that long as well.

In our case, we found a rental house via the Internet. It wasn't in the location we intended to finally settle, but it had the space we needed, a yard for our dog, and was an immediate base in France (the idea of trekking around looking for apartments that would accept our dog didn't have appeal).

Ironically, we fell in love with the area we'd found by pure chance. One thing led to another, meaning we started looking at houses, and as we were about to give up, we found a house in a nearby town and here we are still.

A Base of Operations Versus Travel

If you want to pack your time away with constant travel, your overseas address will shift with your luggage. The alternative is to find an overseas base of operations that you can use like the hub of a wheel, traveling periodically from there. Both situations have benefits and drawbacks and your plans may include a combination. For example, travel around when you begin your adventure to find the location you prefer, then rent long-term there to see if it suits you. If you don't like it, you can move on. If you do, you can simply hunker down for an even longer stay, as we did.

The Travel Option

Forget about having a base if you intend to travel more than half the time. You'll be paying for that long-term base location, plus you'll have to pay for the hotel or other accommodations when you're away from home. In effect, you're having your cake, but losing it too, by doubling your costs.

Also, if you're traveling far afield, it's less time-consuming and less expensive to go in a loop than to have to keep returning to a base that may be out of the way.

If your idea of adventure is to see all you can see, and you have a limited amount of time, you'll probably be smart to plan a route and find a series of places to stay. This does not preclude staying in one place for a month or more; it just means you won't be tied down to a long-term rental or purchase.

The Base Advantage

One big benefit of having a base overseas is the psychological comfort of having a "home" to return to. A base overseas helps you avoid the full-time burnout of constantly living out of a suitcase. You can make shorter visits of a weekend or a week to various locales. One very practical advantage to having a base is that, if you're not moving about constantly, you can take more clothes for different seasons. (After spending one March shivering because I emphasized warm-weather clothes in the initial packing, I discovered this has tremendous value.) When you travel from your home base simply take one bag for schlepping about and hopping on and off buses and trains. You can return for reinforcements when you wish.

Also, there's a certain comfort to having a familiar place as you adjust to the foreign environment. You'll know where to go for medical treatment, the best chocolates, or the friendliest bar. You'll meet people more easily and make friends in the neighborhood. There's a difference between being transient and immersing yourself in the culture. And, financially, long-term rentals are less expensive than the usual tourist accommodations.

These things considered, let's look at some options for finding either temporary or full-time housing affordably overseas.

TEMPORARY ACCOMMODATIONS

Hotels/Motels

Hotels are hotels are hotels. Except, there's a big difference in price between the large hotels with rooms you can reserve from the States and the smaller, family-run hotels overseas. The latter are more interesting for far less money. However, since they are small and personally run, these hotels won't show up on a travel agent's computer. You'll need to find the small establishments through special guide books, or even better, friends who have stayed in the location and rave about "that little place in Bologna for just $30 a night."

By the way, if your destination is in Europe, most country's hotel ratings are not necessarily based on cleanliness or quality, but by the amenities offered. For example, a place may be in a prime location and perfectly wonderful but have no elevators or twenty-four-hour service at the front desk (it's family-run, remember). So it will have fewer "stars" than a place that offers concierge service. If you can do without the pampering, you'll find charming hotels for less cost. Ask to see a room before you take it, and you may be pleasantly surprised.

Bed and Breakfasts

Rooms in private homes are often less expensive than hotels. They offer the added benefit of personal attention from your hosts, who will provide tips about area sights and restaurants.

Overseas, bed and breakfasts go by different names. In France they're called *chambre d'hote*; in Portugal, *quarto*; in Spain, *casa particulare*; and in Germany, Austria, or Switzerland, *zimmer*.

Your travel agent probably won't book them for you (no commission), but you can find books listing them before you go. The Karen Brown series is an outstanding example. We've always been happy with the places we've stayed—from an eleventh-century chateau to a converted abbey to a simple farmhouse complete with a country farm dinner.

You can usually get names of local bed and breakfasts from the tourist bureaus located near the center of the city. In some locations, small street signs point them out.

Hostels

Most people think of hostels as only for travelers in their teens and twenties. Though hostels are popular with this age group and fit their tight budgets, most hostels are open to any traveler. Hostels offer basic accommodations in dormitories for men and women, though some now offer regular rooms for couples or families. You may need to bring a sheet with you, or you'll have to rent one at the hostel.

You can get information on hostel locations available through American Youth Hostels (don't let the name throw you; it's for adults too).

Contact them at 1009 11th St. NW, Washington, DC 20001; telephone (202) 737-5537. Room rates are approximately $18 for members; the membership costs $25 a year. Rooms are about $21 for nonmembers, per night.

Camping
Camping is extremely popular in many areas overseas and offers an affordable, enjoyable option for the outdoor type. I admit to not being one of these, but don't let my own prejudice for four walls throw you. Actually, many campgrounds overseas are extremely well-equipped with showers, washing machines, pools, restaurants, and so on. They cost about $10 to $30 a night in Europe. You can find lists of campgrounds in travel books. Overseas tourist bureaus can provide information, or you can watch for signs along the road as you drive.

One way to have your home and drive it too is to rent an RV in Europe. You can park it in campgrounds, as above; then pick up and drive off when you're in the mood to move on. You can rent RVs from most major automobile rental companies, including Avis, Hertz, and AutoEurope, plus local rental agencies.

LONG-TERM ACCOMMODATIONS

When you decide to stay in one place for several months or more, long-term housing cuts your costs considerably over tourist accommodations. Not only is the average nightly rate less, but generally you'll have more space and a kitchen, so you can cut down on expensive restaurant meals.

Apartment/Home Rentals
If you want to find an apartment or home to rent overseas before you leave the States, start several months in advance. Find a large newsstand that carries papers for your destination and check the classified ads, or have anyone you know at your destination copy those pages and send them to you. From the classifieds you can get a general impression of prices based on the descriptions of the number of bedrooms and amenities. Not being there, however, you can't see the places in person to gauge relative value. Even though two descriptions sound the same, there may be reasons why one two-bedroom apartment is $200 less a month than the other—for example, decrepit plumbing or a bed that wouldn't support a flea (or worse, does!).

We rented a furnished apartment which is too small for us to work on art, our purpose for being here, so I rented a studio as well, but it works for us. And we're here. That's what's important.
—Trish, 50, Paris, France

If you know anyone in the locale, they may be able to scout out possibilities. You can request photos, which helps, but be aware that camera angles are chosen for the best views and your next-door neighbor may be a factory.

Several international message boards list holiday homes and apartments, many of them from individual Americans who use the places part-time and rent them when they aren't there. Write them and ask for photos and information on the local area. In searching for our place overseas I selected three people with possible lodgings from Internet messages. All were glad to send photos, and eventually that's how we chose our first rental.

You'll see ads for apartment/home brokers in various travel publications and on the Internet. They handle home rentals and can help you find a place long-distance, but this method is more expensive, since you're paying for the service of the middleman, and brokers usually handle only the more expensive (as in more commission) places.

Another way to find housing overseas is to make a trip right before moving to find a place to live; then return to the States and pack up. Most people we know visited their destinations to get a general idea of what was available, at what price. We did the same thing on vacations to our destination but didn't make a specific trip right before moving for one reason: We hated spending the airfare when we were going to be there permanently in a few months. Also, most places advertised for rent are available immediately. If you find a place on an exploratory trip, chances are it won't be available unless you leave immediately—or you'll be stuck paying an extra couple of months' rent to hold it while you close up shop in the States.

All in all, it is easier to find lodgings for a few weeks and take your time finding a good value for the long term. Check local classified ads and bulletin boards, ask other expats, or find a rental agent. Once you're on-site, you'll see what you're getting for your money.

When you look at houses and apartments to rent, ask exactly what is included. Often, lodgings overseas are not furnished as completely as you expect. Kitchen appliances, in particular, may not come with the deal. If they are not provided, you must furnish your own by buying new or finding good used ones. Of course, you could purchase used or new appliances, then resell them when you leave. Look for bargains on bulletin boards in supermarkets or train stations.

In some places overseas, apartments or houses come without kitchen appliances, sometimes without the counters even. And in Europe you often have to buy closets; there aren't a lot of them built in. Those are a shock to the system for a lot of Americans coming to Europe.
—Doug, 43, Basel, Switzerland

Home Exchange

Exchanging your home with someone else overseas can save you both the high cost of renting at the new location. Sometimes the deal even includes the use of cars or bikes, plus arrangements to meet neighbors and friends of the people you've exchanged homes with. You can arrange home exchanges through friends of friends, classifieds, or professional home exchange directories or agents. You'll find many exchange offers on the World Wide Web and in travel magazines and newsletters.

Naturally, you'll want to trade references with the person you're exchanging your home with, though there are some who claim that since they're in your home and you're in theirs, it's of equal concern. True, but nevertheless, be thorough in checking financial and personal references . . . and set the parameters in advance about the length of the exchange, whether car or bikes or boat are included in the offer, and how many people will be using your home (personally, I'd weed out the couple with six-year-old twins who were diagnosed as pyromaniacs).

Here are a few home exchange services, including both the "traditional" paper-based exchanges and an Internet-only service.

INTERVAC. This agency covers more than fifty countries, with residences from apartments to mansions. The rate for purchasing the catalog or listing a home varies depending on the service provided. The company also covers house-sitting and rentals to some extent and provides hints on preparation, insurance, and exchanging references. For information: INTERVAC U.S., P.O. Box 590504, San Francisco, CA 94159; telephone (800) 756-HOME, (415) 435-3497; fax (415) 435-7440; e-mail: IntervacUS@aol.com.

International Home Exchange Network. This is a Web site specializing in listing home exchanges and private rentals. You can post your home and review other offerings. If you see something that interests you, you'll handle the negotiations yourself. The site also offers hospitality arrangements (the owners host you while they're still in their home) and vacation rentals. The network charges $29.95 for a year's membership. For information: www.homexchange.com; email: linda@ihen.com.

HomeLink. The HomeLink directory is published five times a year and includes about 15,000 listings, of which approximately 75 percent are overseas. A membership fee of $83 includes the directories and allows you to list your home for free, or add a photo for $18. For information: Vacation Exchange Club, Box 650, Key West, FL 33041; telephone (800) 638-3841; Web site: www.swapnow.com.

House-Sitting

People who live overseas tend to travel on vacation more frequently than in the United States. Of course, they get at least six to eight weeks' vacation. They also tend to leave for longer vacations. A month is not uncommon. Along with extended vacations comes the normal concern of leaving a home unattended. Housebreaking is a rising problem in many areas and owners would prefer a reputable person be in the home to give it that lived-in look.

This is good news for you if you can connect with the right person, and you are willing to curtail your own schedule enough to meet the responsibility of house-sitting. You will live in the home and oversee it for several weeks or months while the owners are away. The "job" may include watching pets or watering plants. We house-sat on Portugal's Algarve for a month one summer. Our job was walking the two dogs (along with our one) and skimming the pool. The maid did everything else. We were very aware of our responsibility, however, and though we enjoyed ourselves, we curtailed our explorations of the area enough to ensure that we were at the house more than away. But, then, with a private pool in August, who's complaining?

Your next question, of course, will be how to find homes to sit. Word-of-mouth will sometimes suffice. One couple in Atlanta has had a house-sitting arrangement in Florence, Italy, for several years running. It's always August when their Italian friends leave and always hotter than blazes, but these two are artists; they could care less about the heat as long as they're near the Uffizzi gallery. Incidentally, if you can house-sit in Europe during July or August, you'll improve your chances of finding a place, since that's the time of year when virtually *everyone* takes vacation.

You might find house-sitting opportunities through friends of friends, the Internet, or by placing an ad in the *International Herald Tribune* or the local paper of the destination you prefer. One monthly newsletter lists places that need house sitters; most of the homes are in the States, but some foreign opportunities are also available. Contact *The Caretaker's Gazette* at 1845 NW Deane Street, Pullman, WA 99163-3509; telephone (509) 332-0806; Web site: www.angelfire.com/ wa/caretaker.

The Biggest Move of All: Purchasing a Home Overseas

Some people who travel to a specific area find they like it well enough to stay for years and decide to buy a home there. The key is that they know the area. Don't purchase a home overseas without having lived in the community at least a year. OK, so we broke this rule. We purchased after six months, but we'd traveled the area for five years on vacations and spent a long time researching, reviewing different properties, and agonizing before making an offer. When we found our place, we knew it would meet our needs affordably and comfortably.

In Portugal, Bob and Anne were object lessons in patience. They rented for two years and got to know their neighbors. As it turned out, they were able to purchase a three-bedroom home in a top location overlooking the Algarve beaches for $80,000, which was way below market value. Why? Because when the house went on the market, the octogenarian American owners were returning to the States and preferred to give Bob and Anne a good deal rather than sell to a developer.

See the locale in all seasons, not just for the obvious reason of weather, but also to note any changes in the character of the community or the neighborhood ambiance. What seems charmingly pastoral in summer sun may seem deathly quiet on drizzly winter nights—or vice versa. You may like a location in winter but discover that tourists overrun it in summer, creating conditions closer to New York City than the bucolic countryside you expected.

Understand the complexities of purchasing property overseas and do not assume anything. You'll be dealing with different laws and customs, and perhaps a different language. If you're to the point of wanting to purchase, search for specific advice in books on the country you've chosen. Contact a qualified attorney and real estate agent. In fact, contact several real estate agents so you can weigh all the comments together and see as many different properties as possible. Often real estate agents don't share listings overseas as they do in the States, so each agent will have different properties.

Also talk to people who have nothing to sell you but know the area well. They will round out your impressions to help you make a better decision. We knew we liked the general area where we bought, but my hairdresser of all people offered a salient comment we realized was valid. She claimed the countryside where we were then renting was *triste* (sad) in winter. Thinking about it, we realized that she was right. All the summer people would be gone back to Paris or London or New York, and the property was isolated. Instead, we bought in a small town nearby and are very happy with that decision.

On the other hand, Gail, a single expat who's been overseas for more than a decade, lives "as far as I can get from town" and relishes the space for a big garden and room to roam with her two very large dogs. She'd hate being where we are, so to each their own.

Before you purchase, know yourself and what you truly are looking for. Don't be swayed by others' ideas of the perfect home. Then be prepared to spend lots of time and shoe leather looking.

I wanted to live the agrarian life. So we bought a
150-year-old farmhouse to fix up. We have acreage to keep us busy for years.
—Peter, 60, Saint Senoch, France

Before You Buy
- Rent in the area first and explore well to uncover the best values.
- Know the weather in all seasons. What's pleasantly cool in summer could be cold and damp in winter.
- Consider the location for ease of transportation, especially if you plan to travel often or want visitors from home. If the house is within proximity to a train station or an international airport, you'll see friends and family more often; whether that's good or bad depends on your penchant for visitors.
- Location affects transportation costs. If gas is expensive, you may want closer access to markets or public transportation.
- Determine how much work you're willing to do on the house. You'll pay less for a fixer-upper, but will have to pay for the labor or spend time doing it yourself. Will you enjoy fixing up that Spanish villa with the stone walls or would you rather take up other activities?
- Have a builder or architect inspect the house before you buy it. Building methods overseas are different and may be difficult for you to evaluate yourself.
- Be sure all the amenities you see are actually included in the price. Don't take anything for granted, since customs are different overseas; frequently people don't leave many things we take for granted here in the States. People have been known to buy houses only to walk in and find nothing but the bare walls—no appliances, no light fixtures, and one expat even found the prior owner had taken the doorknobs.
- Electricity and fuel costs are often more expensive overseas so check that the home is well insulated and has an affordable heating system.

> *On one of my vacations we decided to try to buy a house, but it took about five years to get completed. People kept running off with the money. I likened our house to a chain letter; if you were at the beginning, you got your house. Luckily we were and took title in 1991. The pool didn't get finished until three years later, but it's still my favorite house.*
>
> —Susan, 65, Caracas, Venezuela

In many locations abroad, books are available that go into much more detail than I can here. If you decide to purchase, research the process thoroughly. *The Living and Working in . . .* (France, Spain, Britain, or Switzerland) series (see bibliography) offers valuable tips, not only on purchasing a home, but on countless other aspects of those countries. Many other books are specifically geared to home purchase in Mexico, Costa Rica, England, France, and other locations around the world. Check your bookstore. Or ask the consulate or other expats at your destination for books they'd recommend. In any case, before buying a home, see an attorney who understands not only home purchase in that location but your own situation as a foreign buyer.

9

Transplanting Family, Fido, 'n' Fluffy

TRAVELING IN THE COMPANY OF
THOSE WE LOVE IS HOME IN MOTION.
—Leigh Hunt

As an adult runaway, your actions will impact more lives than your own. If you're married, presumably you and your spouse will be running away together. (If you're just plain running away, it's called divorce.) The challenge will be to ensure that you both are eager for the adventure.

Your move will affect children still living with you; even the ones who are grown, gone, and proud of their independence may suddenly feel deserted. You may have grandchildren. Your aging parents or other relatives may rely on you for emotional or material support. And, you may have loyal four-legged members of the family.

Your decision to leave the States will affect all of these loved ones to greater or lesser degrees. As an adult "runaway," you'll want to handle the transition responsibly, helping them accept and enjoy the experience, whether they travel with you or share the experience vicariously through correspondence.

In our case, we waited until the last child was completely on her own. We also stayed for our parents, since they were in ill health. We're glad we did because we would have been concerned about them, and I'm convinced that the extra time to dream, plan, and budget helped the adventure proceed as smoothly as it has.

You don't need to be impatient. If you can't take your adventure for three, five, or seven years due to family concerns, make the waiting years enjoyable and beneficial. Learn a language. Explore potential locations from your armchair. Make a network of contacts. The years leading up to our getaway were actually some of the most enjoyable, as we looked forward to the adventure.

Your Spouse

You've shared life together for years and take it for granted that wherever you go, your spouse goes. Until, that is, you discover your husband has no interest in giving up hamburgers or his regular golf game—or your wife can't imagine living without a walk-in closet or her bridge club.

Often, one spouse—and it can be either half of the pair—will have the itch for adventure overseas and the other couldn't care less. Then, diplomacy must prevail. Sometimes, the one who wants the adventure can gradually convince the other, though an all-out campaign usually backfires, with the couple polarized. If one prevails over the other despite misgivings, the result can be disastrous for the trip and the marriage. So ensure that you are both looking forward to the adventure, even if one of you is more thrilled than the other.

My husband and I actually flip-flopped in this regard. When I talked for years about wanting to go to Europe, even just for a vacation, his refrain was, "I haven't even seen the States yet." We finally took a two-week vacation in France together, and after that he ate those words. We returned each year for five years for short vacations and finally decided to take the leap. Then I was the one who had second thoughts! At that point, he was the positive one, and I'm glad he was. This adventure together has been a wonderful joint venture, giving us both new interests and opportunities to enjoy life.

Rita Mahoney, director of Prudential Intercultural Services, which prepares corporate employees for overseas moves, suggests that

> The spouse should have positive expectations and be willing to grow and learn the new language, the new cuisine, whatever is required. However, it's also a danger if they're too optimistic. They should be realistic and understand that this will be a different standard of living and they'll be away from family. Otherwise, the shock will hit them too late, when they're overseas.

We're both still enjoying life overseas so we haven't yet faced a hurdle that several people have: Though both wanted the trip initially, one eventually wants to return home and the other wants to stay. It can, and has, broken up marriages. In one case, after two years on a boat in the Caribbean, the husband wanted to stay, but the wife missed her children and grandchildren. The woman came back to the States; the husband didn't. The marriage may have broken up in any case, but I would recommend that you be aware of the potential problem and talk it out before you leave.

Discuss the move over and over again between yourselves. We went through gallons of coffee for months—heck, years—planning and talking everything over. If one of you has serious doubts, visit a marriage counselor for a few sessions. Not that your marriage is bad, but because this is a serious decision and a professional may help you clarify your plans and set the parameters so you both enjoy the experience.

We raised two daughters overseas. Without question it was a good experience. Kids learn to adapt and it opens their eyes to a whole new world of different cultures. Now grown, one daughter has found her niche in international marketing, with a wonderful job and great salary.
—Steve, 51, formerly Switzerland and Africa

CHILDREN

One of the advantages of waiting until midlife to run away is that your children have flown the coop. You don't have the additional concerns of finding a good school and helping your child adapt to another culture. However, if you do have a child still at home, it's still possible to go overseas. Families have enjoyed the adventure together, and executives and military personnel are transferred overseas every year with their families. They not only cope, they often thrive. Their children have the opportunity to learn more about the world in a month than their peers learn in years stateside.

If you have children still living with you, the options for their education depend on age and your family situation. You can take your children with you and have them attend public or private schools overseas. You can leave them with family to attend school in the States, which is often the best option if they are in high school and want to graduate with their friends. You can send them to boarding schools in the States or overseas. Or you can take a year's study program with you and undertake home schooling overseas.

Younger children will adapt faster to overseas life. They'll learn the language sooner and more fluently than adults. It can be difficult to take pre-teens and teenagers however; they're at the stage where they want to fit in, and they'll be the strangers overseas. They won't want to leave friends and activities at their school. This is true even when families move within the United States, and the problem is compounded when moving to a vastly different environment overseas.

According to Rita Mahoney of Prudential Intercultural, children raised overseas are "TCKs" or third-culture kids.

They aren't American, and they're not the new culture, whether it be Spanish or French or Italian. They're a hybrid that creates a third culture. It's up to the parent to understand this and be aware of the changes in the child that occur as a result.

> Our fifteen-year-old granddaughter asked if she could come down and go to school for the year to learn Spanish. Now she's enrolled in a Venezuelan school and is adjusting well. She's busy with tennis two afternoons a week, private tutoring three days. If you were to ask her how she liked Venezuela, she would tell you that she likes the scenery . . . the guys are fine!
>
> —Susan, 65, Caracas, Venezuela

Educational Possibilities

Living overseas is one of the best educational experiences your children can have. Nevertheless they'll need some form of formal education. Below are some means to provide it. Whichever you choose, investigate to ensure that your child will meet requirements when he or she returns to a U.S. school. Make sure that any program you enroll your child in will meet the standards—and that the credits will be accepted. This is especially vital if your child intends to return to the States for college; if your child will attend high school overseas, investigate the entrance requirements for colleges or universities they want to attend.

International Schools

International schools are located wherever there's a large multicultural community big enough to support it, usually, major cities overseas, though I was surprised to see an international school on a dusty hillside in Portugal's Algarve. With the large British and German populace in that tourist area, perhaps that's reason enough for a school in that location.

International schools attract children of expatriates, business people transferred overseas by their corporations, diplomats, and local students who want to concentrate on language studies or prepare for a parent's move to another country. Classes are held in several different languages, and cultural adaptation is part of the process.

These schools are financed by private tuition, so they are costly; but they can be excellent, especially in preparing the older child for the international baccalaureate, which offers rigorous training and is highly desired by some colleges. For more information on schools overseas, contact the Office of Overseas Schools, A/OS, Room 234, SA-6, U.S. Dept. of State, Washington, DC 20520; telephone (202) 875-6220.

I'm glad I gave my kids the experience of living overseas.
The whole world is home to them and now that they're grown,
they think nothing of going wherever the opportunities are.
—Barbara, 47, Florence, Italy

Local School System

If you are moving to a country whose language your children speak, they can enter the local school system. If they don't already speak the language, they can still go to school, but they'll need special tutoring to manage classes and language learning at the same time. This could be stressful, and you may want to start your children in an international school until they adapt.

School schedules overseas differ from their U.S. counterparts. For example, in some countries, students have Wednesday off but attend school a half day on Saturday. The methods of learning are different, and the emphasis in government and history will be of the country you are living in.

Extracurricular activities are different as well. Your student may be disappointed to learn that sports, music, and special-interest groups are not a normal part of the school day. Locate a club or extracurricular group for sports, music, art, or other cultural activities.

The benefit of attending a local school, if the child can manage, is that they become proficient in the language quickly. They make friends within the new culture and gain a broader perspective of the world.

Boarding Schools

Boarding schools are more popular overseas than in the United States, drawing students from countries around the globe. Students should be independent enough to be away from their parents. When one American was young, she attended boarding schools in England while her parents traveled to South America. Eventually she adapted, but was very lonely, even though her sister also attended the school. "I just felt bad for my brother because he was alone at the boys' school," was her comment. If your child is willing and able to handle living away at school, this is an option.

You may want to consider boarding schools in the United States, especially if your child is deeply involved in a sport, such as American-style football or baseball, which would not be available overseas.

Home Study Programs

Correspondence schools make it possible to teach your children yourself. People who never leave town do it, so you can too; but this is a serious commitment, which requires preparation and qualifications on your part. You must have the proper materials and be disciplined enough to see the education through.

For more information, contact one of these correspondence schools:

Kindergarten Through Eighth Grade
The Calvert School, 105 Tuscany Road, Baltimore, MD 21210; telephone (410) 243-6030.

High School Correspondence Courses
University of Nebraska, Lincoln, Division of Continuing Studies, 269 Nebraska, Center for Continuing Education, Lincoln, NE 68583.
American School, 850 East 58th Street, Chicago, IL 60637; telephone (312) 947-3300.

> *My mother is still living, age ninety, and it's very difficult for her to have me down here. But we talk every week and she's still able to live in her own apartment in senior citizen housing. My life here would end abruptly if I had to go back and take care of her.*
> —Susan, 65, Caracas, Venezuela

ELDERLY PARENTS

One of the most difficult decisions for expats is to leave elderly parents. Whether you leave now or wait is a highly personal decision and depends on the health of your parents and the support systems they have available. In our case, our parents were in such bad health that we wouldn't have felt right leaving them for a long period of time, so we settled for vacations and used the time to plan.

Some people choose to take parents along, which, if they're healthy and willing, may be an enjoyable option for you both. One couple built a small house for her widowed mother on their property, and she now basks in the pleasures of French country markets and meeting expatriate friends from Britain, New Zealand, and Germany.

In some countries with inexpensive service economies, such as Mexico, Costa Rica, or Portugal, caring for elderly parents can be more affordable and offer the option to keep parents at home longer than in the States. However, the change in environment may not be acceptable to some elderly people who are set in their ways and would be uncomfortable or frightened by the major changes involved in language, medical care, and culture, not to mention the travel itself. One couple brought a parent and discovered they were limited to taking an hour or two away from the house unless they found a sitter. The elderly woman didn't speak the local language, and they were afraid to leave her longer.

Another woman, a ninety-year-old, talked about going with her daughter and her husband to live in France, but after the couple bought their French home, Mom decided against the move. The husband is now in the house there, while the wife is still in the States trying to reconcile the two responsibilities.

If you're fortunate, your parents will be like those of some friends in Portugal. Both sets of parents are still relatively young and healthy and are vying with each other for the guest room.

The "Family" with Four Legs

Finding a temporary home for Fido or Fluffy in the United States makes a lot of sense, especially if you'll be traveling a lot overseas. Think about grown kids or friends as potential loving homes.

But if you'll be staying put, you may decide to take your pet with you. We did, and it was especially easy since the country we chose, France, is well-known for its love of dogs. Folly has discovered the joys of sitting in cafés with us—along with the delights of occasional treats from various admirers at nearby tables. As for us, after ten years together, having our best friend with us in France went far toward making us feel at home.

Pet Aboard!

If your dog or cat is under seventeen pounds you may be able to bring it aboard the airline in a pet carrier as carry-on luggage. We did this with our dog and found that it was easier than we'd thought. In our nightmares we saw him barking nonstop for eight hours, with the stewardess and passengers tossing us all out over the Atlantic, but he never let out a peep. Outside of two young girls who discovered him while we waited to board, we doubt anyone knew there was even a dog on board. He settled down and slept most of the trip.

A carry-on pet carrier must be of a size to fit under the seat, just as carry-on luggage would, and it should be preapproved by the airline. One approved carrier that's particularly well-designed (probably because a stewardess designed it for *her* dog) is the Sherpa Bag. The bag is made of heavy-duty nylon with mesh panels for ventilation, has an adjustable shoulder strap that doubles as a leash, and a zip pocket for the important papers that accompany your pet. We keep doggy treats and hand wipes in there too. The bag's soft sides make it easy to fit places a hard-sided carrier won't. The Sherpa Bag is recommended by the Humane Society and many veterinarians and approved by several airlines, including Air Canada, Alaska, America West, American Airlines, Continental, Delta, Northwest, TWA, United Airlines, and US Air. You can find the bags in good pet shops or order them from Sherpa's Pet Trading Company, 357 East 57th Street, PH, New York, NY 10022; telephone (800) 743-7723.

Preparing Your Pet

Prepare your pet to be in a carry-on carrier (or cargo version for a larger animal) for the long hours of a flight overseas. Start early to help your pet adjust; don't just expect to thrust him into the carrier and tote him along.

We bought the carrier three months before our planned departure. Folly didn't want anything to do with that strange object on the floor, but we placed doggy treats just inside the door. He stretched his neck out like Ichabod Crane to get the treats without getting inside the carrier. Gradually, the treats went farther inside and so did Folly. At no time did we force him into the carrier. Eventually, we were able to pick him up and place him gently inside, without closing the carrier door. We repeated this until we could close the door. We'd leave him in there to get used to it. After he adjusted to the carrier on terra firma, we picked it up and practiced walking around with him. The final test was a visit to the mall, where there would be crowds comparable to airports. We wanted to ensure that he wouldn't bark or be anxious, and all seemed well.

The real test came the day of the trip. Pun though it is, Folly passed with flying colors.

Canine Cargo

If your pet is larger than seventeen pounds, he'll have to travel in a hard-sided carrier in the pressurized cargo hold. A cargo kennel must be large enough for the animal to stand, turn, and lie down.

Check with a veterinarian to ensure your dog or cat is healthy enough for air travel. Some species have problems flying due to their respiratory systems, so you will want to ensure this is not a problem for your pet. Plus, the USDA requires that your animal be at least eight weeks old and fully weaned in order to be transported on the airline.

Claire and Dick took their two much loved, but large dogs to Portugal via kennels in cargo. The dogs went on the same flight, using the expedited service that many airlines have developed for pets. All went well and Carmen and Cosmo arrived in fine health, though a bit jet-lagged.

Health Regulations

Check with the consulate or embassy of your destination country for specific regulations on bringing a pet. At the very least, you'll need to show that all essential immunizations are up to date. Usually dogs and cats must have been vaccinated against rabies at least thirty days prior to entry; otherwise the pet will have to be kept confined on arrival for at least thirty days after the vaccination date. Carry a valid rabies vaccination certificate and keep it with your pet. Carry an extra copy in your baggage as well. The date of vaccination should be no more than twelve months prior to arrival—even if your dog has had the three-year rabies shot.

Most countries require an international health certificate from your veterinarian. The certificate must be executed within a set number of days immediately prior to travel. In some cases, it must be issued no more than ten days, sometimes within three days, before departure. For our destination, we had to take Folly to the veterinarian for the health certificate within three days prior to the flight. Check with the consulate and airline for exact regulations based on your destination.

We had no problem with the flight in that regard. Our airline, Delta, checked all the pet papers thoroughly before boarding. On arrival at Paris we sailed through customs.

However, some destinations forbid animals to enter at all or subject them to a lengthy quarantine. These destinations are normally islands that have strict regulations to avoid the introduction of rabies. England requires a six-month quarantine of dogs entering the country, a rule which even most Brits consider unduly harsh. It is currently under study for revision, but nevertheless you would not want to take a dog there. Other islands, such as Hawaii and Ireland, though not quite as strict, also have tight regulations. If you're traveling with your pet, don't even take a flight that has one of these locations as an intermediate stop.

TIPS FOR TRAVELERS WITH PETS

Travel Arrangements
• Make the flight arrangements for a direct, nonstop flight.
• Make the flight arrangements for your pet at the same time you make yours. The airline will allow a maximum of one or two animals in the passenger cabin per flight, so you must reserve in advance.
• Make sure the airline knows if your pet will travel as baggage or cargo.
• Avoid crowded times, such as holidays.
• Avoid extremely hot or cold weather. For example, go early morning or late evening in summer.
• Buy a good carrier or kennel of the proper size for your pet. Purchase this through the airline or at a pet store, but if you buy at a store, make sure you get one the airline approves.
• If your pet is traveling as cargo, label the kennel "Live Animal" in large letters.
• Tag the kennel clearly with your name, address, and phone.
• Take food and water for your pet.

Preparing for the Flight
• Reduce or cut out food for your pet twenty-four hours before departure.
• Eliminate water several hours before departure.
• Walk your dog or cat thoroughly.

- Tranquilizers are usually not recommended by veterinarians, unless your animal is very nervous. In fact, sometimes they can have the opposite effect. Our vet explained that one cat went frantic after given the tranquilizers. Getting over them can be worse than the trip.
- If you're concerned about "accidents," one well-traveled owner recommends disposable diapers. She doesn't actually diaper her dog; she puts several together to create a cushy and absorbent lining on the bottom of the pet carrier.

10

Leaving the Roof Over Your Head

TO REMAIN YOUNG ONE MUST CHANGE.
—Alexander Chase

The traditional image of a child running away from home shows the little one with a bundle on a stick. The modern child might carry a backpack to run away. But as a grown-up, you need a Mack truck.

After decades of accumulating possessions, our most difficult decisions when running away as an adult involve what to take, what to leave, and what to do with what's left.

Your home, as probably your most important investment, is central to the decisions you'll make. Within those walls are family memories and mounds of belongings—more possessions than you ever thought possible when you were a child. The big question is: What should you do with your home? Will you sell? Rent? Find a sitter? Close it up and let it sit idle?

Many factors enter into your decision. Primary among them is the length of time you intend to be gone and what you intend to do when you return. If you plan to be gone for a relatively short period of time, even up to a year, and you'll return to the same hometown, you'll probably want to keep your home. It's a major investment and to simply sell it and buy a new home later could be costly.

If you're an empty nester thinking of moving to a smaller home anyway, you might prefer to sell your home before you leave, to avoid the hassles of managing it while you're gone.

Below are some options to consider, along with some of the various pros and cons involved.

> *An older daughter and her husband moved into our house, made the low mortgage payments, and took care of our Siberian husky during the two years we were gone. They were building a house at the time so the timing was perfect.*
> —Susan, 65, Caracas, Venezuela

Is There a Sitter in the House?

By far the easiest way to leave your home is to have someone you trust live there while you're away. This ensures that the house will have a lived-in look, that someone will be around to water the plants, care for pets and the lawn, and handle problems before they become major. You can leave furniture in place, avoiding expensive storage. Having a sitter watch your home also provides the comforting thought that you'll have a familiar place to lay your head any time you return to the States.

This solution works well if you know someone very responsible, whom you trust with all your things. Perhaps you have an adult child or a trusted relative or friend who would love to live in your home free or for a small stipend while you're gone, in return for caring for it.

One woman who ran away to the south of France had the bravery to turn her home over to her architect daughter, who used the house as her project and renovated it for Mom (with her permission, of course) while she was gone.

In any case, when you leave your home, be sure the person watching it is responsible and leave explicit directions on operating all the mechanical systems in the house. Tell the person who'll be living there how to handle any plumbing or electrical problems that may arise and what to do if the washing machine breaks. Provide names of your usual repair companies and any applicable warranties.

The person in your house should have your full itinerary in case of serious questions, but often problems can't wait, so it's a relief to know the person living in your home is familiar with it and will handle things the way you'd want them handled. Leave a small checking account in your name and your house sitter's, in which you put a sum of money for utilities or repairs that can't wait.

Closing Your Home

Some people turn the key in the front door and leave. To ensure your home's safety, however, requires advance planning that protects the home's mechanical systems and ensures that it's not a sitting duck for break-ins.

Have a neighbor or two you trust keep an eye on things. If you don't already have a burglar/fire alarm system, consider having one installed. Make sure the neighbor knows how to deactivate it to check on the house or stop the siren if it goes off accidentally, as these things do.

Put a few lights on timers. Your outside lights can be fitted out with motion detectors. Hire someone to care for the yard on a regular basis and ensure that the mail and papers are picked up daily. You should stop the mail and papers, but marketers leave flyers and free papers on the door or the mailbox anyway, and you won't want these cluttering up the house and proclaiming its emptiness.

Unplug all appliances, including televisions. After you clean out and shut off the refrigerator, leave the door ajar to help it air out. Shut the water intakes to your washer and dishwasher, since the rubber gaskets in these have been known to let go. Shut off water outside too, especially if you'll be gone over the winter. In cold climates, shut off all water to the house and drain the pipes, unless someone will be using the house while you're gone.

Leave the thermostat set at fifty-five degrees in the winter to prevent frozen pipes. If you live in an area that is hot and humid in summer, you may also want to ensure that someone adjusts the thermostat so the air conditioner will occasionally come on to keep the mildew out of carpets and furnishings.

Your homeowner's insurance should protect you while you're gone, though there may be a limit for an unoccupied house. Check this before you go to ensure that your protection doesn't lapse.

The Rental Option

One advantage of renting your home while you're not using it is that the rent can help support your adventure. If you've owned the house a long time, your monthly payments may be lower than what your home would bring in rent. Renting it for more than it costs provides a nice little stipend every month to finance life overseas.

If you have a mortgage, you'll continue to build equity in the home—and with the renter's money if the rent covers the payment. Plus, in case of inflation, you'll have a home to return to that you can afford. If property values go up drastically while you are gone, an equivalent house could be out of reach when you return. Or interest rates may rise, doing the same thing.

Renting is a compromise solution that gives you an "out" if you decide to return to the house. It made a nice transition for us, because I couldn't bear selling our home—until we knew that we'd found something we preferred overseas.

Finding a Renter

Take plenty of time to find responsible tenants. Do a thorough background check. You can find renters by placing an ad in your local paper, or you can check with the personnel departments at large companies nearby. They may be transferring someone in who is looking for a home to rent.

You could also work through a real estate agency that provides rental services. Their fees depend on how much work they do, whether they simply find a renter or actively manage the rental by collecting rent, paying bills, taking care of repairs.

If you don't go for professional management, at least have someone nearby—a friend, relative or neighbor—collect the rent and check on the home occasionally.

Review all mechanical systems in the house with your tenants before you leave. Label the fuse box and tell them how to shut off the outside water in the winter. Don't rely on their memories: Write out special instructions, including a list of your preferred repair facilities, and leave the paper with them. People have a lot on their minds at moving time and having that paper provides a refresher course months later, when they finally have to shut off the water or remember which repairman knew how to fix the balky furnace.

Leases

A lease is a necessity. It will protect you from a tenant's sudden whim to depart while you're thousands of miles away. Get copies of leases from office supply stores, real estate agents, or books on managing rentals. Be sure that whatever lease you use includes a security deposit of more than a month's rent in case the renters move suddenly or damage the property. Also request the last month's rent in advance and, of course, the first month's rent.

The lease should limit the number of people living in your home and indicate whether smoking, redecoration, or pets are permitted. Note who is responsible for paying the utilities such as gas, electric, garbage pickup, pest control, cable TV, and who must do the yard care. If you prefer to ensure that any of these are managed to specific standards, for example yard care, then arrange a rent that's large enough to cover these extra costs. We left our lawn-care equipment for our renters, but they chose to hire a professional lawn service. I must say, our lawn never looked so good.

Make it clear how repairs are to be handled. Your renters may be able to handle them up to a certain dollar amount, perhaps $50. After that have them contact you or your representative. Be reasonable however. The hot-water heater died for our tenants two days before Thanksgiving. Our son-in-law in charge of the house had already left for the holiday. So the tenants charged the water heater and had it repaired, providing the bill to our son-in-law. He checked it over, and we reimbursed them.

Tax Write-Offs for Renting
Renting your house may enable you to write off certain expenses. Among other things, the advertising required to find a tenant, insurance, mortgage interest, property taxes, management fees, and repairs are all tax-deductible. You can even depreciate the house and furniture in it.

However, if you depreciate the house, the depreciation can be taxable as capital gains later when you sell the house. Definitely consult a financial advisor, since the paperwork or expense for depreciation may or may not be worth taking depending on how long you intend to be gone, what your house is worth, and other factors.

Should You Rent Furnished or Not?
In our suburban area, it was recommended that we rent our home unfurnished, since most people wanting that type of home were business people who already had their own furnishings. The opposite may be true if you're in a college town (but don't leave your best things there).

If you rent furnished, you'll cut down on outside storage costs, since the home itself will store your belongings. But even if you rent your home furnished, don't leave valuable or personal items out. Store them in a lockable closet or room, a rented storage locker, or leave them with family or friends.

Whether you rent your home furnished or unfurnished, make a complete survey and inventory of the home, noting its condition and its contents. You and your tenants should sign it. Then keep a copy and give a copy to your renters.

> *Once committed to making The Move, we gave up our*
> *apartment and moved in with a friend for the last year in*
> *the U.S., putting personal belongings into storage.*
> —Anne, 61, Albufeira, Portugal

Selling Your Home

Selling your home is the ultimate move. It means breaking all ties with your neighborhood and determining once and for all that you will not be returning to that house. You may return to the States, but not to that exact home.

This is one decision to make with a clear head. Don't let the excitement of your adventure carry you overboard. However, if you've considered selling your home anyway, then this may be the ideal time to divest yourself of the responsibility of a home that is thousands of miles from where your adventure takes you.

There are many reasons to sell at this stage of your life. The home could be far too large now that the kids are all gone. The yard may be more work than you want. You may want something in a different part of town—or eventually you'll be retiring to a resort community.

Don't sell your home to pay for the getaway itself. Investing the money can provide peace of mind because you'll have the money to purchase another home when you return. But be aware that selling may incur a capital gains tax if you haven't lived in the home the required number of years. Whatever you do, see your accountant or tax advisor before committing to selling your home.

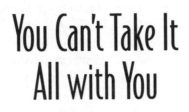

11

You Can't Take It All with You

HE WHO WOULD TRAVEL
HAPPILY MUST TRAVEL LIGHT.
—Antoine de Saint-Exupéry

Leaving on an adventure means leaving behind your favorite armchair, different outfits for every day, and your collection of antique widgets. Console yourself in the fact that you'll collect experiences far beyond the material things you left. After all, you don't really want to reach the end of your days and say, "I sat in my chair" or "I looked like a fashion plate." Chances are you'd rather say, "I lived an interesting life and still remember that year in Tuscany."

Once you face the fact that you can't take it all with you, your job is to consider what you will take and what to do with the remainder.

I've spent the first half of life accumulating
things. The second half, I'll accumulate experiences.
—John, 62, Loire Valley, France

Take It, Store It . . . or Do Away with It

Starting several months before departure, your mind should be buzzing with the possibilities for all the things you own. The options for any item break down to taking it with you (or shipping it later), storing it, or getting rid of it by selling it or just plain giving it away.

Some decisions are easy. The worn-out rug the dog threw up on goes in the garbage. Other decisions are more difficult. Will you really use that massive armoire, and is it worth the money to either store it or ship it some-where overseas?

In our case, we weren't sure how long we'd be away, because we had decided to try our adventure for a year, then reevaluate. If we returned, we'd need furniture, and replacing it would be costly. However, we knew we would downsize eventually, so we compromised by getting rid of furniture for the den, a grown daughter's room, and the guest room. As it turned out, we guessed right because what we had left later fit nicely in our (smaller) home in France.

What you're doing with your home will impact on your decisions. In our case, we gave our kids some of our things (televisions and the VCR proved popular), and our tenants agreed to let us store the remaining fur-niture in one section of the basement. That eliminated storage fees. We later moved the belongings when we bought our house overseas.

Decide what you will do with everything early. It takes longer than you think to arrange sales—even longer to get the kids to pick up the moth-eaten varsity jackets that they don't wear but won't let Mom throw out. You won't want to be picking through all this at the last minute. If you do, the decisions will be forced upon you, increasing the chances of your making a mistake and later regretting what you've kept or not.

> *We sold nearly all our belongings, including the house, but taking*
> *our two beloved dogs, Cosmo and Carmen. As the house [in Portugal]*
> *was furnished, there wasn't much need to ship household belongings . . .*
> *except the rototiller. Dick had to have the rototiller!*
> —Claire, 45, Algarve, Portugal

The Giant Sale Solution
Making a major life change like a sabbatical or retirement overseas is a good time to clear out the extra junk—especially if you plan to store your furni-ture or sell your house. You won't want to pay storage for things you don't intend to use again, and you can use the cash for your getaway.

Consider, also, that rooms are often smaller overseas than in the wide open spaces of the United States. Unless you already have a house and know the rooms are spacious, beware of taking king-size beds, extra-large sofas, or oversized tables that may not fit.

After struggling with a narrow stairwell, our movers, in typical French fashion, conferred for several minutes, then hoisted a sofa bed and enter-tainment center onto the top of the moving van, backed it up to a window and used a ladder to bridge the gap, finally putting the items to rest in our second floor, whereupon all parties shook hands in celebration—and relief.

Relentlessly "clean" house, starting with a giant garage sale. If you've already made an exploratory trip and intend to run away for several years, you may want to sell everything. Several couples who moved to Mexico chose to do this because it was too troublesome and expensive to move everything and furniture is cheaper in Mexico, so they simply used the money from the sale to buy new furniture.

On the other hand, replacement costs of the things you sold second-hand will be costly when you return. Apply common sense and consider your own plans carefully.

> *We did a fairly major sell-off of furniture and belongings in the*
> *U.S. to raise money for a year without income. If I were to do it again,*
> *I'd do the same. Starting over in a foreign country forces you to adapt quicker.*
> *You have to go shopping, negotiate delivery of furniture, etc. You come*
> *to terms with different ways of doing things.*
> —Doug, 43, Basel, Switzerland

Donations

After you've done your best to reap a profit from the belongings you can't use anymore, you may want to give items away to family or friends. We've made some people very happy with lamps and small appliances that we didn't want to cart to Europe.

Many items can be donated to charity, and you can take the value as a tax deduction. Most people use this as the last resort for all the things that didn't sell at the garage sale, and charitable groups such as Goodwill are more than happy to have your cast-offs. In fact, a charity's representatives will often call you; the smart ones follow on the tails of your garage sale ad! Remember to get a receipt for the donation. The records will be needed when you file your tax return.

WHAT TO DO WITH THINGS YOU CAN'T DO WITHOUT

Is There Room in the Family?

If you have family or friends with extra space, and they're willing to store your furniture in a clean, dry area, you're all set. This is the most economical alternative to selling your possessions, and you'll know your things have a happy home.

Even if your family can't take all your belongings, they may be willing to keep special mementos to avoid putting them into a storage locker. If they keep the fragile or expensive items, you can at least save money by getting a smaller storage locker or one that isn't climate-controlled.

Professional Storage

Storage units come in sizes suitable for everything from a few boxes to huge rooms capable of holding a houseful of belongings. They range from basic garage-type units for self-storage to climate-controlled units. For important items, especially furniture or art, be sure the storage unit is climate-controlled. This will be more expensive than a regular unit but will limit damage from mold and mildew and temperature extremes.

We put our things in storage, but didn't buy a house right away.
Then we used the shipment money to live, so now we're using the
furniture that came with the house . . . but I miss our stuff!
—Anne, 61, Albufeira, Portugal

Sample Storage Fees. To give you some idea of how storage units compare, here are some sample sizes, types, and the prices per month.

Size (in Feet)	Regular Units	Climate-Controlled
10 by 10	$90	$115
10 by 20	$130	$185
10 by 25	$150	$235
10 by 30	$185	$300
15 by 20	$185	$300
15 by 25	$225	$375

You'll pay a deposit for the unit. If you pay a year's rent in advance, many places will negotiate a discount. When you look at the prices you'll see why the garage sale comes before anything else.

When you decide to store furnishings, put pencil to paper to see if it's cheaper to store your belongings than to ship them. Your decision will depend on the length of time you'll be away, your plans for returning, and the type and amount of belongings.

One couple stored their belongings at a cost of $160 a month, although they would have preferred to have their own things in their home overseas. That was three years ago. They've already spent $5,760 on storage and lived without their things. The cost of moving would have been about $7,000.

On the other hand, moving furnishings immediately doesn't make sense when you're unsure how long you'll be gone. Live with a furnished rental or find second-hand stuff overseas until you can make an informed decision.

Our furniture was too good for this primitive style of house so we didn't
move it. We made furniture and did all the work on the house ourselves. A
friend even painted murals mimicking Portuguese tile motifs.
—Mary, 61, Moncarpacho, Portugal

An Electrifying Truth

Check the electrical requirements at your destination. If the electricity differs from that in the United States, which uses 110 volts, you'll need adapter plugs, plus converters or transformers for anything electrical you take.

In addition, the hertz, or cycles per second of the electrical system, may be different. For example, North America uses 60 Hz; Europe uses 50 Hz. Since converters and transformers do not convert cycles, appliances with motors may run faster or slower.

Some things, such as televisions and VCRs, won't work at all in certain countries overseas, because the actual broadcast or tape systems are different.

Gizmos and How to Use Them

You've heard of adapters, converters, transformers, and the like. If you've never had to use them, here's a brief description of what they are and when to use each.

An adapter plug attaches to the U.S. plug, enabling you to plug your appliance into the wall outlet, which will be of a different shape overseas. This is purely a question of size and shape. The adapter will *not* convert the electrical voltage or cycles.

A *converter* can convert power for an electric appliance (for example, from 110 to 220 or vice versa). Converters will work for short-term, high-voltage use on simple appliances, such as hair dryers, vacuum cleaners, coffee makers, and so on. As a general rule, they work for appliances that don't have to be kept plugged in regularly. Check the manufacturer or supplier of your converter to see what they recommend.

Do *not* use a converter with electronic items. Even mundane products, such as a programmable clock radio or toaster oven, could have electronic parts these days, so be careful that you don't assume wrongly. Anything with an electronic component requires a transformer.

A *transformer* will enable you to use electronic appliances such as computers, copiers, or fax machines. A transformer works with either electric or electronic products, so if you're unsure, choose the transformer over a converter. Buy the proper size transformer, based on the wattage of the appliance. Check with the manufacturer of the transformer to see what one will work with the electronic appliance you intend it for.

You can purchase adapters, converters, and transformers at travel stores and electronic shops, such as Radio Shack or through catalogs such as Franzus, (203) 723-6664; Magellans, (800) 962-4943; or Walkabout Travel Gear, (800) 274-4277 or (800) 852-7085.

I was impressed with Walkabout Travel Gear's customer service. They provide complete information on electric current requirements overseas and helpful advice about what you need to adapt. You can download a complete electricity index from their Web site (www.walkabouttravelgear.com/wwelect.htm) or e-mail them at walkabouttravelgear.com.

The Great Lamp Debate

There are two schools of thought about taking U.S. lamps (110 volts) overseas, where the power is 220 volts.

According to some people, adapting U.S. lamps of 110 volt and 60 cycles for use on other voltages and cycles is a bad idea. The wiring is a different gauge. Also, U.S. lightbulbs are not compatible with 220-volt use.

However, some people in Europe replace the bulb with a 220-volt bulb and use a plug adapter. It's worked, though I can't recommend it. Some experts I talked to felt that the switches and materials may fail under the higher voltage.

The best advice I can give is that, if you want to take a particular lamp overseas, go ahead, but have a specialist there examine it to be sure it will work safely.

You can use a transformer on a lamp; however, when you consider that you can buy a lamp just about as cheaply as the transformer, it seems like a drastic solution.

Consider all of the above when you're deciding what to take, sell, give away, or store. Obviously, it's a waste to move electrical appliances unless you can adapt the power successfully. You'll have to buy new (or new to you) overseas to replace them.

Your Car

Before you decide to ship a car overseas, check import regulations and fees at your destination. Certain car makes may be forbidden. At the least, cars will need an entry permit and often will need modifications to meet overseas emission or safety standards.

Finally, check whether parts and service for your car, and the type of gas your car uses, are readily available at the destination. You'll also need to consider the right-hand versus left-hand driving problem if you're going to a destination where people drive on the "other" side of the road.

Frankly, I think the only reason to keep your car is if it's paid for and you're leaving for a short time, say six months or less. If you'll be gone a year or more, you'll be much better off selling your car. Otherwise, you can store your car, but it will cost you unless you find a relative with extra garage space. You'll have to insure it as well, unless it's not driven. All of which adds up to extra expenses. Invest the money from selling your car in a good used one overseas—or simply in your trip if you can get by overseas without a vehicle.

Just like all rules, this one can be broken for valid reasons. Some friends of ours kept their car because they kept their home and just left their car in the garage, with adult children watching out for both. The advantage to keeping their car is that, when they return for visits, they have wheels. We, on the other hand, have to rent a car like tourists. That's expensive, but we didn't want to keep up the insurance and find storage just to have a car for visits.

*My advice? Don't move a car. We brought our station wagon overseas but
the roads and parking are narrower, and a smaller car would be easier to drive.
On top of that, the regulations here call for this little "e" on the headlights. They
don't make a size to fit our car. We're still fighting the system . . . and still
getting stopped for having 1996 Olympic plates!*

—Pam, 52, LeMans, France

MOVING LOCK, STOCK, AND KITCHEN SINK

Once you've decided to make the expat experience last several years you
may want to move your belongings. People who've done so report, for the
most part, that the experience went smoothly. Overseas moves aren't that
different than moves within the States—except your belongings travel farther, and usually in a ship's container, rather than a moving van.

You can hire movers to pack your things, or you can pack yourself, but
I don't recommend the latter. Movers won't insure belongings if you pack
your favorite crystal yourself. You can ship enough to fill a twenty-foot container for about $7,000 to $7,500, which includes the cost of everything
except customs duties. It will take approximately four to six weeks for your
belongings to reach you from the time they're picked up. The exact amount
of time will depend on the distance, the transportation, and the time
needed to clear customs. The moving company will provide a formal quote
and give you an estimate on the scheduling.

International Moving Companies

If you have friends who've moved overseas, ask what company they used
and if they were satisfied with the service. Call several companies for an
estimate. You can find movers listed in the Yellow Pages. International
movers have local representatives throughout the United States who are
listed locally, or call the national telephone number to find the representative near you. Be sure the mover has international moving experience and
tracks your shipment from start to finish.

A few of the larger international moving companies with 800 numbers
and/or Web sites to check are

United Van Lines, One United Drive, Fenton, MO 63026; telephone (800)
325-3870. To help families adjust to a foreign culture, United offers programs for adults and children on adjusting to the new location.

Allied Van Lines, Web site: www.alliedvan.net/. This Web site will help
you find local agents. It also provides tips on moving.

North American Van Lines, Web site: navl1.com/. As with most international movers, they rely on local agents, so see your Yellow Pages.

Vanpac International, 1340 Arnold Drive, Suite 231, Martinez, CA 94553-4189; (800) 877-0444; e-mail: sales@vanpac.com; Web site: www.van-pac.com/.

Estimates Are Essential

Call several movers who specialize in international moves for estimates. Their representative will visit you at your home or wherever your belongings are stored to see everything that you plan to move. The representative will estimate the cost of the move, including labor and packing materials. They will tell you the most efficient way to move the quantity of goods you want to take, for example, a twenty-foot or forty-foot ship's container.

We learned the hard way to compare estimates of volume as well as price. We chose a well-known international moving company, and our house was rented, with our belongings stored in the basement. We knew what the price should be, and when we got our estimate, we simply agreed, not wanting to "bother" our tenants by traipsing through more than was necessary.

Our sad tale was that the sales representative underestimated our goods, telling us we had more than enough room to fit everything in a twenty-foot container. Well, around midnight moving day, a quarter of our belongings were still strewn around the pitch-dark driveway. A week later, after partially unpacking the container at the warehouse, sorting through things, giving away, throwing away, and throwing up our hands in despair, we settled for an extra crate to be delivered later for $2,000 more.

If we had had more estimates, one probably would have said we needed a larger container and that would have given us a clue that there was a problem.

The Paperwork of Moving

The estimate, sad to say, is not always binding. If the mover packs for you, the final bill will depend on the actual weight of the load, which determines the packing charges. However, you will have a good idea of what the weight of the load is based on the volume of the container, which is estimated.

When you have the estimates, call your Better Business Bureau and Consumer Protection Agency to see if the mover has a good reputation. In comparing the estimates, check that the movers are supplying the same services and insurance. Unfortunately, some movers may "lowball" you to get the order, by undercounting items, so make sure everything is included. Check that the quantity of packing materials is basically the same if you're using their packers. See, also, how many men they plan to use. A smaller crew may look less expensive, but if it takes more time it will cost more in both your money and frustration.

Check the insurance coverage. This is often inadequate, and at the last minute you might discover your belongings aren't properly covered unless you buy the optional extra insurance. When comparing estimates make sure you know exactly what is insured and for how much.

Inflation is an amazing animal, and that table you bought for $50 ten years ago could now cost you $200 to replace if it's broken. Always base your insurance on the current replacement value. On the other hand, if you buy optional insurance, and an item has little value, beware of insuring it too heavily.

Cash First, Shipping Later

International movers often request full payment before they will ship your belongings. Be prepared and ask what form the payment should take—for example, if they require a cashier's check—so your shipment isn't delayed. Our mover neglected to mention that the full amount was due before they'd move the container (yes, this is the same representative who also underestimated the load in the first place!), so we assumed payment would be on delivery. At the last minute we had to make a frantic call to our broker to wire the funds or our shipment would have been put on the back burner.

How Your Belongings Will Travel

Metal Ship's Containers

The normal mode of overseas moving is via metal ship's containers that hold a household full of furniture. The containers are transported by truck or rail to the port, where they are loaded onto a ship for the closest seaport, then reloaded onto a truck overseas and delivered. These containers are specially designed to offer protection against the elements on the ship's crossing.

Ship's containers come in standard sizes of twenty or forty feet. A twenty-foot container holds approximately 1,100 cubic feet, which translates to about 8,000 pounds, or enough for the belongings for an apartment or small three-bedroom house. The forty-foot container, of course, holds double that. If you have a large home or want a car shipped, you'll need the larger size. The approximate cost for a twenty-foot container is $7,000; a forty-foot is about $8,500, depending on weight, shipping locations, and destination.

Wooden Lift Crates

If you have less than a full container load, your belongings may go in a wooden lift crate, which is used for smaller shipments of about 200 cubic feet, normally under 4,000 pounds. You may actually share a ship's container with another person's belongings, though your belongings will be packed in their own crate.

Sharing a container load can cut your costs of shipping considerably, although you may have to be more flexible as to delivery dates, since the partial container may wait days or even weeks to be completed. The partial container will be loaded into a ship's container with other shipments, or it can be sent by itself to some destinations, if for some reason the destination can't handle a ship's container.

Air Freight

Smaller parcels can be sent via air, in special corrugated cardboard containers ranging from 5 to 100 cubic feet in order to fit into the aircraft doors.

PACKING

It's generally recommended that the movers pack your things, for both insurance and import reasons. If the movers do the packing, the boxes will be marked "Mover Packed," and you'll have an easier time getting through customs on the other end. Apparently, the customs officials figure you won't have been able to smuggle that Rembrandt as easily if the moving company did the packing for you.

You can pack your things yourself if you want, but use the professional methods and ask the moving company to have their packers open the boxes to check the packing. If they do this, they can mark them "Mover Packed."

While the packers are working, stay around to keep them on their toes. They should pack every item, including putting mattresses and box springs in special cartons; mirrors, artwork, and other fragile items should all be specially cushioned.

Tips for Packing Yourself

If you pack your belongings yourself, use professional methods to improve the chances of everything arriving safely.

- Label the contents on every box, noting in which room the box belongs.
- Mark fragile boxes on every side.
- Leave clothes in dresser drawers (ask your mover first, however; some prefer them packed in boxes).
- Use several inches of crumpled paper in the bottom of each box that contains fragile items; then wrap each item individually with lots of paper cushioning around it.
- Wrap plates, saucers, and china individually. Then bundle the dishes in groups of three or four.
- For especially delicate objects, pack one box inside another to further cushion the contents.
- Check to see all caps are secure on liquids.
- Do not pack flammable materials or aerosol products such as hair sprays, shaving cream, insecticides, cleaning products, nail polish remover, bleach, lighter fluid, or motor oil.
- Ask the mover for blank newsprint to use to avoid the smudging of newspaper.

• Purchase specialized cartons for books, china, and wardrobes from discount moving supply houses. You can also purchase blank newsprint paper.

CUSTOMS REGULATIONS

Storage is not included in the mover's fees, so it's up to you to ensure that customs arrangements have been made properly at the destination, enabling your belongings to move directly to your new home.

Check with the consulate or customs office at your destination to find out the exact customs regulations. If any items you want to bring into the country are questionable, obtain written assurance from the consulate that the item can be admitted.

What Can and Can't Be Admitted

You can take your household belongings duty-free into most countries, but most have regulations that do not allow you to bring in articles less than a year old. This enables people to bring things for personal use but discourages people importing goods for resale.

Most countries have a list of items that are not allowed to be imported at all. Usually, you should avoid taking liquor, tobacco, pornographic materials, flammable items, precious metals, cameras, or unexposed film. If you want to bring your camera, bring it on the plane with you, though I must admit my old collection of cameras got packed in the bottom of a box and made it fine.

Many countries prohibit handguns and other weapons. Those which are permitted will require permits. Don't include any weapon in your shipment without written approval from the consulate. Ammunition is prohibited due to the risk of explosion on board the ship or plane.

Houseplants, seeds, or bulbs cannot be shipped into most countries. If you want seeds and they're permitted, check for a special permit; then carry the seeds with you.

Destination Delivery

The moving agent should give you the name and phone number of their agent at your overseas destination. Once you arrive there, contact the destination agent to make sure they have the correct address and phone number in order to contact you immediately when your shipment arrives. They will also send you some forms that need to be filled out to get your belongings through customs.

If you're moving a ship's container, the overseas moving agent should be able to give you an estimated arrival date at the port though they won't be able to tell you the exact delivery date at your house until the shipment has cleared customs.

THE OVERSEAS MOVE

Three to Four Months Before
- Sort household goods; have a garage sale or otherwise dispose of things you don't feel are necessary overseas.
- Make storage arrangements for things you want to keep but aren't moving.

Eight to Twelve Weeks Before
- Collect estimates from three movers; select one.
- Set a packing and moving date.
- Draw a floor plan of your new home so you know what to take.
- Determine what to take and what to leave. Evaluate if electrical appliances will work in your new home overseas. If not, leave them or buy adapters, converters, or transformers as necessary.
- Make travel reservations.
- If you have school-age children, get copies of their records and arrange to send them to the new school.
- Get copies of medical and legal records from doctors, dentists, veterinarians, lawyers, and accountants; ask for referrals if possible.

Four Weeks Before
- Begin packing household goods, if you are packing yourself. Start with things you don't use daily.
- Get change-of-address forms from the post office and mail them.
- Open a new bank account overseas, if necessary, and transfer funds for use when you arrive.

Two Weeks Before
- Call utilities to set the date for cancellation.
- Start gathering and packing the things you'll take on the plane.
- Gather important papers, such as wills, insurance papers, stock, and titles, and store them in a safe place or take them personally in your carry-on luggage.

Two Days Before
- Have mover pack goods, unless you've already done it.

Moving Day
- Read the bill of lading. Keep it until everything is delivered safely.

Delivery (Approximately Four to Six Weeks Later)
- Be available to answer questions on delivery.
- Have money available in the local currency or check in case of unexpected expenses, such as a customs charge.
- Note on the inventory any damaged or missing boxes to later make a claim.

12

Personal Packing for Runaways

LESS IS MORE.
—Robert Browning

Imagine those college students who take off for a year overseas. They don't need much more than their backpacks. As an adult, spoiled by years of comfort, I wouldn't narrow my packing that much, but I do think that you should avoid being bogged down by belongings on your sabbatical.

How much is too much? Naturally, it depends on how long you'll be gone, where you're heading, and your activities once you're there. When we traveled on vacations for three weeks overseas, we'd brag that we could do it on a carry-on and backpack. However, traveling to live overseas for months or a year does require a few more belongings. You should be able to do it, however, with two to three large bags; some people can do with less.

At first it seems as though you'd never be able to fit everything in those three bags, but it's plenty, especially if your destination is in a warm climate. A lot more shorts fit in a bag than heavy sweatpants. All bets are off if you need to pack parkas.

If you plan to remain in one place, like Portugal's Algarve or Mexico, where the weather is relatively consistent or mild year-round, you'll have an easier time packing than for four-season climates. The biggest problem is packing enough for a change of seasons or locale requiring different clothes. Packing in this situation can be done, however, with layering, which we'll talk about later.

Most airlines allowed two carry-on bags, but the carriers are now becoming stricter. Check your airline's latest regulations before you pack. When we left the States, we were fortunate in being able to take a backpack (with notebook computer inside) as one carry-on. My husband's carry-on contained important papers, a camera, an address book, a paperback for the plane, and so on.

We also had our dog, whose carrier came along as an extra-cost piece of baggage but was allowed in the passenger compartment with us. Because we had all this, it was even more important to minimize our actual wardrobe cases, so we each checked two of them. That was it. In any case, check with the specific airline for exact regulations regarding the size and type of luggage permitted.

How to Dress for Months Away Without Taking a Steamer Trunk

Layer, Layer, Layer
Take clothes that work with one another and also work under and over each other. You can layer a collared shirt with a sweater, then a windbreaker. By layering you can handle everything from spring through fall in most climates.

Take Lightweight, Easy Wash and Dry Clothes
Jeans are comfortable friends for casual trips. Unfortunately, they're also the bulkiest clothing item you can take and the worse to wash and dry quickly. If you must take jeans, limit them. Chinos or other cotton/polyester blend pants are much more practical for men or women. They can be worn during the day for touring or made presentable for casual dinners out.

It's sometimes difficult to find clothes that combine all the benefits of lightweight, nonbulky fabrics that are washable and fast to dry—and have pockets for secure storage. Some catalog companies specialize in travel clothes with all these benefits. One of them is TravelSmith at (800) 950-1600. Their clothes for men and women fit a range of climates but are light, easy to pack and wash, and wrinkle resistant. My husband's particularly proud of the nylon cargo pants he found, which dry quickly, need no ironing, and have legs that zip off, converting them to shorts.

Mix 'n' Match
Take clothes whose colors blend easily with each other. This simplifies layering and provides countless additional combinations of outfits. Do not take special outfits in which only one shirt works with one skirt or pair of pants. Avoid special-purpose clothes, such as a special dress. For men, a sport coat works better than a suit, since the coat can be another layer for warmth or dressed up with a shirt and tie.

Make Clothes Do Double Duty

Women can take a skirt and blouse that match, to look like a dress, but can be worn separately or together for dressier occasions. Something as small as a pair of earrings can dress up a casual outfit. Opt for versatility whenever possible.

A large T-shirt works with pants or as a sleep shirt. Sweat pants snuggle into cold sheets and work as exercise wear during the day. Slip-on shoes are casual daywear as well as handy slippers. Think like this and every possibility is covered.

Stick to Middle-of-the-Road Styles

Choose clothes than can be worn casually or for dinner, with a change of accessories. For example a sweatshirt will always be a sweatshirt and can't be worn except for a very casual occasion. But a neat pullover sweater can work during the day and be decent for casual dinners out as well. Jeans are also too casual. Chinos work well during the day or night for casual dinners. Short shorts aren't as practical as longer ones or culottes for women, which can be presentable for touring or at a resort.

I recommend shirts with collars, especially the kind called "club shirts." The collared shirts are more presentable than T-shirts, and they layer nicely with sweaters or under a sports coat.

One Large Rolling Bag Works as a Luggage Carrier

It's hard enough negotiating airports without having to carry heavy cases, especially if you need extras such as a backpack or dog carrier. Using a large roll-about bag as the base, you can carry another bag, by stacking a smaller case onto it. By pulling these two pieces and wearing your backpack, you can get yourself around easily.

The variety of sizes in bags is important because, once overseas, you can then use the smaller bag or the backpack, which is multifunctional, for weekend trips.

Cheat with a Backpack

A backpack comes in handy as an extra carry-on piece. Put your prescriptions and important papers, checkbooks, camera, and so on in it and never let it out of your sight. You would never check any of those things anyway. Once you're overseas the backpack comes in handy for carrying maps and your camera when wandering around, leaving your hands free to check out those wonderful handcrafted products. You can cycle wearing a backpack and the pack can double as a beach bag, picnic hamper, or shopping bag for small purchases.

Two Bags for Six Months: Packing for Runaways

Wardrobe/Women

- Five club-style shirts that wash easily and dry
- Two T-shirts for sports and sleepwear
- Three skirts or pairs of pants
- Shorts (depending on your destination)
- One blouse and skirt combination for dresswear
- One neutral-colored belt
- Poncho or lightweight raincoat (preferably with hood)
- Heavy coat, hat, gloves (depending on destination)
- Three sweaters (two casual pullovers, one cardigan-style as cover-up for dresswear)
- Seven pairs socks or hosiery and underwear
- Three pairs shoes (two for walking, one pair for dress, or sandals, depending on destination)
- Bathing suit
- Hair dryer (with voltage changeable from 220 to 110)
- Costume jewelry (to dress up casual skirts without taking much space)

Wardrobe/Men

- Five club-style shirts that wash easily and dry
- Two T-shirts for sports and sleepwear
- Three pairs of pants
- One pair shorts (more for warm-weather climates)
- One nice shirt-and-tie combination
- Sport coat
- One neutral-colored belt
- Poncho or lightweight raincoat
- Heavy coat, hat, gloves (depending on destination)
- Three sweaters
- Seven pairs socks and underwear
- Three pairs of shoes (two pairs good for walking, one pair dress shoes or sandals, depending on destination)
- Swim trunks

Additional Items for Men and Women

- Toilet articles
- Sunglasses/extra prescription glasses/contacts
- Electrical plug adapter for foreign electrical outlets
- Medications/copies of prescriptions
- Address/date book
- Travel alarm
- Watch
- Reading material
- Camera/film
- Compact umbrella and/or plastic raincoat
- Special needs (tennis racket, swim goggles, art supplies, etc.)
- Traveler's checks/records (keep records separate from checks)
- Credit card records
- Travel itinerary and travel books

And Don't Forget

- Passport/visa
- Tickets
- Birth certificate
- Marriage license
- Photocopy of your passport ID page (keep separate from your passport)
- Credit card, bank card for automatic withdrawals/traveler's checks
- Driver's license/international license
- Special IDs: insurance card, auto, health, other
- Pocket dictionary for foreign language (if needed)

Extras

- Notebook computer
- Diary/pens/small calculator
- Pet carrier/pet supplies
- Measuring cups/spoons (if you can't handle metric overseas)
- Favorite recipes (ditto above and for language reasons)

Remember, You Can Always Buy It Overseas

People overseas have to live there too. You can buy products overseas, so you don't need to pack everything. Just take an initial supply of toiletries until you find new brands you like.

The only exception is for those items you know to be extraordinarily expensive where you're headed, or even unavailable. Pack extras for use until you get settled and find substitutes, or have visitors from the States bring them. Most expats have at least one thing they require guests from the States to bring as their price of admission.

> Start making lists of the things you will want to buy
> [in the States] before you leave ... favorite sundry items, even
> insignificant things like dog toys and insect repellent. I actually started
> stockpiling things six months in advance to take advantage of sales
> and spread the acquisition costs over a number of months.
>
> —Claire, 45, Portugal

13

Passports, Visas, and Other Bureaucracies

FOR MY PART, I TRAVEL NOT
TO GO ANYWHERE, BUT TO GO . . . THE
GREAT AFFAIR IS TO MOVE.
—Robert Louis Stevenson

You won't need a passport if you're running away to a U.S. possession, such as the U.S. Virgin Islands, but for most other locations around the world you'll need one. Most countries also require a visa if you plan to stay over sixty or ninety days.

Passports

Applying for a Passport
Your passport is issued by the United States government, to tell the world that you are a U.S. citizen. You must have a passport to travel most places outside the United States.

You can get a passport application from certain post offices and courthouses, or even over the Internet. To apply, you must show proof of citizenship, including your birth certificate, so be prepared with the original documents. You'll also need two clear two-by-two-inch pictures of you, taken within six months of the date of your application. The pictures must be taken against a light-colored background, with you looking straight at the camera; don't try for that side angle, even if you think it's more photogenic.

You can have passport photos taken at most photo studios, or use one of those photo machines that are ubiquitous in shopping malls.

Take the completed passport, supporting documents, and photos to a passport agency or a post office that is designated to accept passport applications (your local post office can tell you which post offices in your area offer this service). Your application will then be sent to one of the main U.S. Passport Agencies, which are located in Boston, Chicago, Honolulu, Houston, Los Angeles, Miami, New Orleans, New York, Philadelphia, San Francisco, Seattle, Stamford, or Washington, D.C. Your passport will be issued from one of these locations and sent back to you.

Leave plenty of time to arrange for your passport. You'll need to find original documents and, even if you have them at your fingertips, once you apply, it can take about three to five weeks to receive your passport, depending on the time of year. Passport offices are especially busy in spring and summer, with people planning summer vacations.

You must have the passport to apply for a visa, so if you need a visa, apply for your passport several additional months in advance.

Simple passport transactions such as applying for or renewing a passport can be handled via regular mail. If you're down to the wire and need the passport within three working days, you can expedite the process by paying a rush fee of $30 and proving your departure is within fifteen days. Naturally, you'll plan your running away far in advance and won't need to rely on this.

Passports cost $65 when you first apply and are good for ten years for those over eighteen years of age. If you're taking children younger than eighteen, they get a five-year passport for $40, which can't simply be renewed but must be re-applied for. Children ages thirteen to eighteen must apply in person, but legal guardians can appear in place of younger children. Even infants need their own passport.

The Consumer Information Center, part of the U.S. General Services Administration, puts out a pamphlet called *Passports: Applying for Them the Easy Way*. Order it by phone at (719) 948-4000, or fax (719) 948-9724 with your credit card number. The pamphlet costs fifty cents, plus postage.

Incidentally, if you plan to travel often to places where you'll need a visa (see the "Visa" section below), you can request a forty-eight-page passport when you apply. This will provide additional pages at no extra charge and ensures you'll have plenty of pages to go around the world. However, most people can manage with the usual passport, which is easier to tuck into a pocket or purse. If necessary, you can have pages added later. Don't do this yourself, however. In fact, don't alter your passport in any way.

Renewing Your Current Passport
If you simply need to renew a passport, you can do it by mail, provided your most recent passport was issued within the last twelve years, and you were at least eighteen years old at that time. For a renewal, send a DSP-83 mail-in form, available the same places as original passport application forms, with your expiring passport, two recent passport photos, and a check or money order for $55.

Also, the State Department has joined the cyber-world, providing passport renewal information on the Internet. You can even download the forms you'll need from the on-line home page of the State Department Bureau of Consular Affairs. If you're a cyber-traveler, check the Web site at travel.state.gov.

Don't assume that just because the Internet takes microseconds your passport will be in your hands faster. If you're in a rush and need a passport for a trip within two weeks, you'll still have to wait or use the postal rush service.

Passport Information Numbers
You can get most passport questions answered by calling the Federal Information Center. The toll-free number is (800) 688-9889; then press five for passport information. The touch-tone messages are available twenty-four-hours a day for general information.

Check Your Passport Expiration Date!
Even if you have a passport, double-check its expiration date before beginning your jaunt. Some countries won't admit tourists with a passport that expires within the next six months, so renew well in advance. You can renew a passport any time that it's valid and for two years after it's expired. After that you have to start from scratch and apply all over again.

Protecting Your Passport
A U.S. passport provides your identification as a United States citizen and is a valuable commodity overseas. In fact, there's a considerable black market for U.S. passports, which, in the wrong hands, can be used for nefarious purposes, so guard your passport well from pickpockets. If you lose your passport, report the fact immediately to the local police and your nearest consulate.

In some countries, hotels will request your passport when you register in order to submit data to local authorities. Ask when it will be returned (usually the next morning) and don't forget to pick it up. Your passport is essential for your travel. We checked into an Italian hotel one time, only to be told that the room was ready but the previous guest had left with his baggage—and the room key. "What if he doesn't bring it back?" we asked. "Oh, he will," said the clerk. "We have his passport." We got the key soon after.

Visas

Unlike a passport, the United States government does not supply a visa to visit another country. The visa, as the State Department defines it, is "an endorsement or stamp placed in your passport by a foreign government that permits you to visit that country for a specified purpose and a limited time."

You may or may not need a visa, depending on the country you plan to visit and the amount of time you intend to be there. Many countries permit tourists to visit for a reasonable length of time, such as a month or three months, using just your passport. However, if you intend to remain in a country for longer periods, say, six months or a year, a visa is usually required. Some countries require visas no matter how short your visit. For a brief list of typical requirements, see below.

Applying for a Visa
To obtain a visa you must give your passport to the country you want to visit, so you need the passport before applying for the visa. The consulate or embassy of the country involved will provide specific details on their regulations for processing a visa application. This requires filling out countless forms and supplying background information detailing your reasons for wanting to stay in the country, your financial condition, and your health. You will need to provide several more photos such as you used for your passport, and you'll pay a fee. It takes several weeks, often months, to get a visa, so plan well in advance.

In most cases you must get your visa in the United States before you leave the States and enter your destination country. Some countries will not issue a visa for you once you have left the United States.

For general information on visas call (800) 688-9889 (the same federal number used above for passport information). Press five, then three for visa information. But for the specifics you must talk to the embassy or consulate of the destination country.

Laws have tightened here. At first all we had to do
was nip across the border into Spain once every sixty days and get
our passports stamped to renew our tourist visas. But when EU [European
Union] border controls were abolished we had to apply for legal residence
or risk fines or deportation. It was no big deal though.
—Anne, 61, Albufeira, Portugal

Destination Entry Regulations
The U.S. Consumer Information Center offers a pamphlet, *Foreign Entry Requirements*, providing entry regulations for over 200 countries around the world. It lists basic information on visa regulations, provides consulate and embassy addresses, and tells you how to apply for a visa. If you want the

publication call (719) 948-4000 or fax (719) 948-9724 with your credit card number (MasterCard, VISA, or Discover). The pamphlet costs fifty cents, plus postage.

Even if you order the *Foreign Entry Requirements* pamphlet in the planning stages, call the consulate or embassy of the country or countries you decide to visit and ask for their *current* requirements. Sometimes entry regulations change faster than the printed materials can keep up with them.

Meanwhile, here's a look at the current requirements for passports and visas in some of the countries you may choose to run away to.

Country	Passport	Visa Required for Stays Longer Than
Australia	Yes	90 days
Austria	Yes	3 months
Belgium	Yes	90 days
Costa Rica	Yes	90 days
France	Yes	3 months
Germany	Yes	3 months
Greece	Yes	3 months
Ireland	Yes	90 days
Israel	Yes	3 months
Italy	Yes	3 months
Japan	Yes	90 days
Mexico	None for U.S. citizens	90 days
Portugal	Yes	60 days
Spain	Yes	3 months
Switzerland	Yes	3 months
United Kingdom	Yes	6 months

(England, Northern Ireland, Scotland, Wales)

Once more, remember that visa requirements can change. When you've decided on your destination, double-check the current regulations with the nearest consulate from that country.

Health and Immunization Rules
Every government wants a healthy populace, so they require immunizations to protect their people from you and to protect you from any health risks in their country.

Ask the consulate or embassy of your destination country if you need special immunizations—for example, against yellow fever, malaria, or cholera—or a proof of health before entering the country. In case of side effects, have your vaccinations several weeks in advance of your departure.

For your own protection, make sure other immunizations, such as tetanus, are current before you leave.

*We frequently ask friends and relatives to send us something from the
States because it's not available or too expensive, but we tell them to clearly mark
"gift" on the package. Otherwise the customs duties can be outrageous.*
—Dick, 52, Algarve, Portugal

Import Regulations

The consulate of your destination country can provide a list of duty-free
items that you are allowed to bring with you or ship later. The consulate will
also list the prohibited items, which might include pets or plants, weapons,
even a knife, lightbulbs, or uncooked meats. Find out the specifics before
you plan to take that arsenal of Civil War rifles.

Illegal drugs will get you in major trouble no matter where you go—
and in some countries can result in nightmare penalties that you wouldn't
dream of in the States. So, just don't do it.

You won't get in trouble over your heart medication, but if you do take
any medications, keep them in their original containers to avoid unneces-
sary questions or delays at customs.

A Note About Bureaucracy

Every country, yes, even the United States, has its bureaucratic nightmares,
and we have heard enough stories to put fear in the hearts of the most foolhardy. But chin up—chances are your road will be smooth if you use common sense and follow the regulations.

Even when the worst happens, it can be worked out by staying calm and
trying a little persistence. In Portugal, Claire and Dick were notified that their
shipping container with all their furniture couldn't be delivered, but would be
stored—the costs of which would support the country for the year—because
their visas were late. They'd applied properly but had to leave the United States
without them. Fortunately they had arranged so far in advance that one of the
customs personnel went out of his way to give permission for the furniture to
enter. They got the visas five months later.

In France, a thirty-something couple entered on their passport, then
remained in the country well past the three-month limit—seven years past the
limit, in fact. It wasn't until they had a minor traffic run-in that they needed to
prove residency. They ended up with a residency permit automatically because
they'd lived there so long. Go figure.

The point of these tales is not to tell you to ignore the system. You could
be the one who gets caught and subject to penalties. So check the specifics
on your destination. Follow the rules and network with other expatriates to
find out the best ways to make the bureaucracy turn from a nightmare to .
. . well, let's just say a bad dream that you wake up from eventually. And
when you wake up overlooking the Caribbean or a vineyard ripe with
grapes or the cobblestone streets of a charming old-world village, you'll
proclaim it all worthwhile.

14

Transportation: Getting There

A JOURNEY OF A THOUSAND
MILES MUST BEGIN WITH A SINGLE STEP.
—Chinese proverb

Although you could hitch on a freighter, let's assume that running away from the United States means taking a plane. So at some point you will need to find a reasonably priced airfare.

There are two problems with airfares when you're leaving the country for a long period of time—going and coming back. Airlines don't set up their best round-trip prices for travelers gone more than thirty days. Sometimes they'll give you ninety days or even a year, but the prices go up in relation to the time frame and freedom you're buying.

I'll give an example of how airlines ticket passengers and make it difficult to travel long-term. When we were planning to fly to Paris the cheapest flight was $950 round-trip if we came back within three months, but we knew we'd be wandering Europe for longer than that. Could we buy a one-way ticket for half that price? Not exactly. The one-way ticket was the same price! A second option was a ticket valid up to a year, for $1,400 each. Ouch.

Meanwhile, a sale appeared with tickets to Paris direct for just $400 round-trip. The only hitch was that the return was assumed to be within a week. It was an easy decision to buy this ticket. We just didn't use the return portion. We took the chance that we'd find another sale or consolidator ticket to return.

If you're going to use just half a ticket, book the return anyway. The airline will require it for the round-trip ticket. However, once you're at your destination and know you won't be using the return half, it's only fair to call the airline and let them know, so someone else can purchase your seat.

Warning: The above works only with your outbound flight. Don't *ever* attempt to use the return half of a round-trip without using the outbound ticket. If you don't show up for the first leg of the flight, your reservation will be canceled completely.

How to Find Deals on Airfares

Travel During Sale Periods
Getting a good price on your flight can be as simple as planning your trip overseas during the off-season, being flexible with your flight times, or making the purchase as far in advance as possible.

We planned to leave in March. The weather would be getting better in Europe by then, but the ticket prices are less expensive than in summer. The best time to buy tickets to Europe is in winter from approximately November 15 to March 15. The next best times are the shoulder seasons of spring and fall, from March 15 to May or September 15 to November. Summer is far and away the most expensive time to travel.

Plan your flight for off-peak days of the week. The most expensive days are over weekends so take the midweek flight. As a runaway, you're not tied to a schedule, so enjoy the savings by being flexible with your time.

Be Persistent
You might not find a sale immediately, but don't give up. Remember those $400 tickets we found? Well, originally the price was based on leaving no later than March 8. Unfortunately, our visas wouldn't be ready until March 15. What to do? Besides panicking, we hounded other airlines, but found nothing even close to that low price. More than a week later, becoming desperate, I called the first airline back. They had just extended the sale to March 15. We had our sale price and the later date too.

Talk to a Travel Agent
A good travel agent can scout out the sales through their handy computers. They can review countless options in airlines, routing, and dates to determine the best tickets for you. They may find a ticket with a stopover that's vastly less expensive or discover that, if you can wait two weeks, an airline will start winter sale prices.

Do-It-Yourself
I often find it easier to call airlines myself in order to compare prices and times directly. If you prefer this method, here is a list of toll-free airline numbers for information, ticket schedules, and reservations.

Toll-Free Airline Reservation Numbers—U.S. Carriers
(for overseas and U.S. connections)

Alaska Airlines	(800) 426-0333
American	(800) 433-7300
America West	(800) 235-9292
Continental	(800) 525-0280
Delta	(800) 221-1212
Kiwi International	(800) 538-5494
Midwest Express	(800) 452-2022
Northwest	(800) 225-2525
Pan Am	(800) 359-7262
Southwest	(800) 435-9792
TWA	(800) 221-2000
United	(800) 241-6522
US Air	(800) 428-4322

Toll-Free Airline Reservation Numbers—Foreign Carriers

Aer Lingus (Ireland)	(800) 223-6537
Aerolineas Argentinas	(800) 333-0276
Aeromexico	(800) 237-6639
Aeroperu	(800) 777-7717
Air Canada	(800) 776-3000
Air France	(800) 237-2747
Air Jamaica	(800) 523-5585
Air New Zealand	(800) 262-1234
Alitalia	(800) 223-5730
All Nippon Airways	(800) 235-9262
British Airways	(800) 247-9297
El Al Israel Airlines	(800) 223-6700
Emirates Air	(800) 777-3999
Iberia (Spain)	(800) 772-4642
Icelandair	(800) 223-5500
Japan Air Lines	(800) 525-3663
KLM (Netherlands)	(800) 374-7747
Korean Air	(800) 438-5000
Lufthansa (Germany)	(800) 645-3880
Mexicana	(800) 531-7921
Qantas (Australia)	(800) 227-4500
Sabena (Belgium)	(800) 955-2000
SAS (Scandinavian Airlines)	(800) 221-2350
Singapore Airlines	(800) 742-3333
South African	(800) 722-9675
Swissair	(800) 221-4750
Thai Airways	(800) 426-5204
Virgin Atlantic (UK)	(800) 862-8621

Ticket Consolidators

Ticket consolidators buy unsold seats from major airlines, then resell them to the public. You can find lists of consolidators in the Sunday travel section of large city papers, for example the Sunday *New York Times*. Since some of these ads could be fly-by-night operations (pun intended!) be sure to verify their credibility before making your purchase. Deal with reputable, licensed IATA (International Airline Transport Association) members.

You can buy consolidator tickets through a travel agent. If the agent deals with consolidators on a regular basis, they'll know who's legitimate. In any case, buy from a consolidator in your locale if you can. That way you can check on them by picking up tickets in person.

Most consolidators charge a service fee (2 to 5%) for paying with a credit card because the bank charges merchants. Despite this, always pay by credit card. That way, if a problem occurs, you'll have some recourse.

You can sometimes get frequent-flier miles for consolidator tickets, but not always. For round-trip tickets, you may only be allowed a maximum of ninety days for travel; if so, this route won't work for longer-term travel, unless you plan to use half the ticket.

One final word of advice: Occasionally, when flights are empty, an airline's fares are lower than the consolidator ticket. Double-check with the airline, a travel agent, and the consolidator before purchasing your ticket to ensure getting the best deal.

Courier Travel

You've probably heard about the good deals available for couriers, who escort packages on flights. They do this by giving their baggage allowance to a shipper; it's less expensive than cargo rates, but since a courier is expected to give up the baggage allotment, this obviously won't work for someone who's going to need more than carry-on for a long adventure overseas. In addition, couriers are usually expected to use the return flight and can't travel with someone else. Forget trying a courier flight unless you're using it for a quick exploratory trip to investigate a destination.

Charters

Tour operators contract with airlines to fly charter flights, which are filled with specific groups. However, when the seats can't be filled, regular people like you and me can hitch a ride with the high school marching band going to Vienna for concert season. Be aware that sometimes schedules and itineraries can change. If the band members all catch the flu, the flight might be canceled at the last moment.

Discount Clubs

Some airlines, American Airlines and Delta for example, offer travel clubs with special discounts to members. Usually the deals are offered based on last-minute travel to specific airports and have a set end date of just a few days later, but if you're flexible on your departure date and want to use just the first half of the ticket, you might find a dirt-cheap deal.

You can often find special airfares via the Internet. American Airlines, for one, offers last-minute specials on international flights, which are posted or e-mailed directly to you when you sign up for their subscription list. There's no charge for this service.

The problem with these types of offers is that they are posted the week during which you are required to travel. You'll have to be extremely flexible about when you leave.

However, such deals may be less expensive than anything else you'll find. If you're ready to go at a moment's notice and are free to hang around a few weeks in case the right deal doesn't appear at first, then you can try it. Otherwise it could prove to be a nerve-racking wait before you can start your adventure.

Frequent-Flier Miles

If you're leaving the corporate world with a pile of unused miles, use those for your escape. Airline partnerships now extend the options for their use through code sharing. For example, Delta's worldwide partners include Aero Mexico, Aer Lingus, TAP Air Portugal, Austrian Airlines, Finnair, Korean Air, Malev Hungarian Airlines, Sabena, Singapore Airlines, and Swissair. That's a lot of choices for your adventure and that's just one airline.

Check Requirements Before Reserving

If you're planning to take an extraordinary amount of luggage or pets with you, check before you reserve your tickets to ensure that the airline will accommodate you. Some airlines will take your small cat or dog in the cabin with you, but they limit the number of pets per cabin on a flight. You must reserve when you buy your tickets to ensure that no one else will get that allotted pet reservation. Fluffy would be very disappointed if promised a trip and then left at the airport or sent as cargo.

Incidentally, don't plan to fly out the same day you close up the house or move belongings to storage. Too much can go wrong at the last minute, so leave yourself some slack. There's no big rush, and a day or two extra before leaving will enable you to arrive at your destination more relaxed.

15

Transportation: Being There

THE MAJOR JOURNEY FOR
YOU IS JUST BEGINNING. FIND JOY
IN MAKING THE JOURNEY.
—Verla Collins

In many countries, the internal bus and train systems are more comprehensive than in the United States. You may find it possible to travel where you want to go, when you want to, without investing in the expense of a vehicle. That said, a car does make it easier to explore the most interesting and out-of-the-way nooks and crannies of a country. Certainly, if you're living overseas for any length of time, you'll want a car for major shopping excursions or sightseeing trips where you want the flexibility not offered by public transportation.

Consider where you'll be living. In the country, you'll want a car. In a large city, most residents do nicely without one, but may rent a car for special outings.

Let's look at some of the choices.

CAR RENTALS

If your plans call for short-term visits of up to a month overseas and you need a car, your best choice is simply to rent. Make the arrangements before you leave the United States because the prices available to tourists from the States are usually better than what you can get from the same rental companies once you're overseas.

Depending on your destination, you could find local companies overseas that will give you a good deal on a car rental. If you have a friend in the locale, they may be able to recommend a company. You can always try the phone book once you arrive at your destination, though I recommend having a car reserved with a major company, if only for the first few days. You'll then have time to scout out the other options without the pressure of standing by the airport curb with luggage and no place to put it.

Brush up on your shifting technique, and you'll save money on the rental. Most cars overseas are manual transmissions. Even if automatics are available, the manual transmission vehicles are less expensive to rent and save gas, which costs a small fortune overseas.

If you insist on renting an automatic, reserve your car far in advance. Here are some U.S. car rental companies with their direct international car rental numbers:

Avis	(800) 228-4369
Hertz	(800) 654-3001
National Car Rental	(800) 227-3876
Budget	(800) 472-3325

Overseas car rental firms that are good to know about include

Kemwell	(800) 678-0678
Auto Europe	(800) 223-5555

Kemwell is known for offering good deals in Europe, so if you must rent long-term, call them first. They offer a "lease," which is actually a pre-arranged deal to purchase/repurchase the vehicle. The leases start at seventeen days and include insurance. But the cost of renting a vehicle is prohibitive if you intend to keep it for several months. You can easily set up your own purchase/resell plan by buying a used car and reselling it later (see "Purchasing a Car" below).

Auto Europe has long-term rentals available, but does not have a purchase/repurchase agreement. An example of the prices: a Renault Clio with unlimited liability, fire, and theft insurance, rented for six months at $23 per day would cost $4,140, for ninety days at $24 per day, $2,160. The rental price includes emergency roadside service throughout Europe.

Recreational Vehicles
Most campgrounds cost $10 to $20 per night in Europe, and many auto rental companies also offer RVs, so if you have a mind to take your "home" with you while you travel, you might want to check out Avis, Hertz, and AutoEurope for their offerings.

Purchasing a Car

If you're overseas for a long period of time and need a car, renting one soon costs as much or more than buying a decent used car.

For example, leasing a car for five-and-a-half months would have cost us about $3,235. Instead, we purchased a roomy Citroën with about 90,000 miles on it, loaded with extras like power windows, radio, and even my favorite "toy," an electronic key chain to lock and unlock the doors, for about $3,000. We're still using our Citroën, but when we sell it we'll get at least something for it, so we've come out ahead by buying.

If you need a car, rent just until you can find an inexpensive but serviceable set of wheels to buy, then sell before returning to the States. If you purchase your car from a dealer, ask if the dealership would be interested in purchasing the car back from you after six months, a year, or whatever. In our case, the individual who sold us our car had a friend who had serviced the car for years and volunteered the fact that the friend would like us to see him first when we were ready to sell.

Before You Buy a Car

- Choose a brand that's popular in the country where you plan to spend most of your time. It's easier to find parts, and service will cost less.
- Get a car with good gas mileage; you'll thank me every time you fill up with gas at $4 to $5 a gallon.
- Consider the type of fuel (regular, unleaded, super, or diesel) and its availability in the country (or countries) you plan to visit.
- Don't buy too large a car. Roads overseas are narrow and parking spaces small.
- Don't buy too small. Make sure you can fit luggage in the trunk for your travels, to hide it from view.
- Buy used. A used car is less expensive, depreciates slower than a new car, and is less tempting to vandals.
- Don't buy air conditioning unless you're in a hot, humid climate where even the natives consider air conditioning essential. Air conditioning cuts gas mileage and is unpopular in areas where gas is expensive, so it might lessen your ability to resell the car quickly later.
- Choose a manual transmission to cut costs.
- Buy a simple vehicle. An obviously expensive or elaborate car will simply make you a target for petty theft.

Driving Licenses and Registration

You can drive many places overseas with your U.S. license. If you'll be relying on your U.S. license, make sure it will be valid for the entire time you'll be out of the country.

In many countries—France is one I know of—you'll have no problem using your U.S. license. In others, such as Spain and Portugal, it's recommended to have the international driver's license, which translates your license into eleven languages and is recognized by hundreds of countries around the world. It's only good for a year, though, so get it at the last minute.

American Automobile Association (AAA) offices are authorized to provide international driver's permits. You don't have to take a driving test. Just take your U.S. driver's license and two passport photos (or AAA will take the photos for an additional $9). The cost of the license itself is $8 for members and $10 for nonmembers. The whole process takes only a few minutes.

I still remember being pulled over by the GNR in Portugal—no reason, just a security checkpoint—but I happened on the one policeman in the Algarve who didn't speak English. I provided the car registration, U.S. license, and international driver's license. They compared all of the above for face and name and apparently decided I wasn't the drug runner or whomever they were looking for.

Incidentally, if you do decide to live overseas for a long time and become a resident, you'll need a driving license for that country. But check out reciprocal arrangements for trading your U.S. state license for an overseas license. In France for example, a South Carolina license can get you a French license without the hassles of driving lessons, which are otherwise required.

I'm better off without a car here. I could only use it every other day anyway, because of the even-odd license plate system for pollution control. I don't know how people who have to get to work handle it, but they do. You just have to adjust.
—Judy, 62, Athens, Greece

Tips on Driving Overseas
Before getting behind the wheel:
• Learn the international symbols for vital road directions, such as stop, yield, no passing, one-way street, and no parking. They're not difficult but essential!
• Learn the systems for navigation. In much of Europe, for example, you drive more by looking for the direction to the town you're heading toward than by the number of the route. This system is actually easy, but may confuse you until you adjust.
• Plan major drives for daylight hours.
• Avoid rush hour and city traffic.
• Reserve ahead in tourist centers or during popular times.
• Buy good maps, such as Michelin maps, and use them.

RAIL

Train travel is common overseas, and therefore the schedules and systems are often better than what you may be accustomed to. You can buy individual tickets or a rail pass that enables you to use the train for a set number of days in a certain country or series of countries. In Europe, the train passes are less expensive when you buy them before you leave the States, so if you know you want to travel by rail, make plans before leaving. For information on Eurail passes, call (800) 722-7151. Travel agents can also arrange for the passes, or you can contact the tourist office of the country you plan to visit.

Once in the country, ask for discounts before you buy a train ticket. Many countries offer lower prices on trains during off-peak hours, discount tickets for seniors, sometimes as much as 50 percent, or provide savings for two people traveling together.

BUS

The typical American shuns buses as a time-consuming and shabby travel alternative. Leave those thoughts back in the States. In some areas overseas, buses are extremely popular—sometimes they're even your only alternative.

For example, Mexico's first-class buses are literally the Mercedes of buses. On longer trips, they provide a snack of a sandwich, chips, and a soft drink. You can relax in plush seats and read or watch videos of movies and entertainment features. Of course, being a relative newcomer to the country you'll probably want to watch the scenery. That's another reason why bus travel is more interesting overseas. You can sit back and enjoy the view, without the hassles of driving.

> *We drive and the cuota (toll roads) are superb highways,*
> *with rest stops along the way with clean restrooms and gasoline.*
> *We've toured in the first class buses and enjoyed every kilometer, watching*
> *television when the countryside didn't offer new vistas. Very cheap*
> *but luxury class, with reserved seats.*
> —Betts, 74, Mexico

16

Staying in Touch

NOTHING CAN COME
BETWEEN TRUE FRIENDS.
—Euripides

Unless you're wanted by the FBI, running away does not include melting into the misty isles of Ireland, never to be seen again.

You'll want to maintain contact with friends, family, or business associates back home. Keeping in touch will, in fact, be a necessity if you have children in college, elderly parents, or investments that bear watching. No matter how much you think you've simplified your personal and financial life, undoubtedly some pesky detail needs handling.

Running away is different than traveling on a vacation, which lasts a relatively short period of time. On vacation you're not concerned about changing your address or having mail forwarded. *You're* the one sending the postcards to friends, not the other way around. But if you're gone more than a month or two, you'll want to receive mail wherever you may be.

The way you handle mail forwarding and other forms of communication with correspondents in the States will depend on several factors: your destination, your access to a postal box overseas, whether or not you'll be at one mailing address or, alternatively, whether you'll be traveling regularly.

MAIL AND HOW TO GET IT

Change of Address

Transferring all mail from the old residence to the new one is the normal system when people move. However, if you're planning an adventure with temporary housing overseas, telling all your correspondents the new address may not be an option at first. We were renting a house for the first four months and didn't know exactly where we would be afterwards. It wasn't worth changing the mail to that address, only to change it again.

We solved the problem by doing the change of address to a PO box in the States for forwarding (for how and why this works, see below). However, if you've already found a specific location overseas where you intend to settle for sufficient time, just supply your new address to friends and business contacts.

Your local post office has change-of-address kits including handy post-cards that you can fill out and mail, with space for your old address, the new one, and the date the new address will be in effect. Correspondents will update their files to send mail directly to your new location. These post office cards are simple and to-the-point. They do the job, especially to magazines and creditors. I might add, however, that magazines may not transfer the subscription overseas due to the increased mailing costs. The international edition of *Time* magazine is more expensive—and smaller!

We wrote personal letters to friends and family informing them of our plans and how to contact us. I say "personal letters" though, in fact, most of us cheated slightly, writing one "Dear Friends" letter on a computer, then personalizing it to the recipient. It's not as warm and fuzzy as an individual letter perhaps, but the move was imminent, and they all needed the same information anyway—what we were up to, where we intended to go, and how to reach us.

Remember to notify the post office itself of your new address. If you forget to tell someone you've moved, the mail will be forwarded to you. The U.S. postal service will forward first-class mail for a year. It will forward second-class mail, which includes magazines, for sixty days. Parcels and bulk mail (third class) will not be forwarded. If you forget to notify someone and mail is forwarded, be sure to notify that correspondent of your new address.

Changing your address with each correspondent is the simplest way to keep your mail coming—and the most affordable. It eliminates the middle-man by having your mail transferred directly to you without having to use a post office box or forwarding service. Unfortunately, this system doesn't work if you'll be traveling or don't know where you'll be living right away.

CHANGE-OF-ADDRESS CHECKLIST

Notify of New Address:

Current post office   _____

Friends and relatives   _____

Credit card companies   _____

Attorney   _____

Accountant   _____

IRS/state tax bureau   _____

Insurance companies: _____

    Health   _____

    Life   _____

    Disability   _____

    Automobile   _____

    Home   _____

Utilities   _____

Banks   _____

Stockbroker   _____

Clubs/professional organizations   _____

Magazine and newsletter subscriptions   _____

Favorite catalogs   _____

Physicians   _____

Veterinarian   _____

Employer's personnel office for your W-2   _____

City/county tax assessor   _____

Voter registration   _____

Drop as Soon as Possible:

Unwanted magazines   _____

Newspaper subscriptions   _____

Annual reports   _____

    (If you've simplified your financial life, you won't need them. Besides, who needs to be notified of an annual meeting three weeks ago in Detroit when you're sunning on a beach in Costa Rica?)

Make a Three-Month "Can't Miss" List
As soon as you know you'll be moving, start to list all your correspondents, jotting down the name and address for eventual change of address notifications. Begin this list at least three months in advance. That way you'll catch communications and bills, such as insurance, that come only quarterly.

Magazines put the address for change-of-address notifications somewhere up front, near the masthead. Cut out your address label from each magazine as you receive it; then simply paste or tape the label to the change-of-address card when you're ready to fill it out.

Remember that magazines (second-class mail) will be forwarded for only sixty days; parcels and bulk mail (third class) won't be forwarded at all. You may be glad to lose that junk bulk mail, but you'll also lose your favorite magazines and specialty catalogs unless you notify the publishers of your new address as soon as possible. It takes several weeks for most magazines to put address changes into effect.

Allow most magazine subscriptions to run out. If you plan your escape enough in advance (which I recommend), just don't renew any magazines or newspapers that would continue after your estimated departure date. Otherwise a relative, friend, or mail service must mail the magazines to you, which is extremely expensive. Magazines are packed with paper—very heavy paper—and most of that is printed with advertising for things you won't need overseas. Besides, with the time delay, you may not get the *Sports Illustrated* swimsuit issue until summer when you're seeing the real thing on the beach at Biarritz or the Costa Brava.

MAIL FORWARDING METHODS

U.S. Postal Service
Your post office in the States will forward first-class mail free of charge for up to a year *if* it's transferred within the United States. You can forward mail to a PO box or friend's house in the States without incurring extra postage.

If you're moving overseas, the U.S. Postal Service will forward your mail, but you will be responsible for the extra postage due for international delivery. Therefore, it's essential to notify your correspondents of your new address, so they can send your mail directly to you. That way each of them—not you—will pay mailing costs.

The post office will put a "hold" on your mail for up to a month. This option may come in handy if you leave to find an apartment and expect to have an address overseas within that length of time.

Naturally, holding or forwarding your mail will delay your receiving it—and delay your receiving all your bills. Nice try, but it doesn't absolve you from paying them. You simply get nasty overdue notices and interest charges. Use the post office to hold or forward mail for only a brief time.

Take a few packs of the post office change-of-address cards with you overseas. When you find that ideal Italian villa, use them to notify all correspondents and send the special card in the pack to your post office in the States. The post office can then forward your mail so that if you've forgotten to notify old Aunt Maude of the new address, she can still leave her millions to you after her cat dies.

Family/Friends

Rather than Uncle Sam, you could take advantage of family or friends—even an attorney or accountant—to forward your mail. They will package your mail and pay postage to forward those packets, and you—I presume—will reimburse them. Send flowers or a gift occasionally to show you appreciate all the work they're doing on your behalf so you can have this adventure.

The trick to success with this system is ensuring that the chosen person is responsible and reliable. The best person is someone who loves you dearly and is settled down in one location. Your older sister who's lived in the same house for twenty years will do. Your college son who changes apartments with the new moon won't.

If you trust the person to judge the value of your correspondence, you can cut the cost and hassles of forwarding unimportant mail. Nothing's quite as irritating as finding that you just paid $30 to forward three annual reports, two real estate solicitations, and the notice from your old subdivision's "garage sale jamboree" held last month.

Tip: Get Gifts, Not Merchandise

If friends or family send packages to you overseas, have them mark them as "gifts," or you may be hit with unexpected (and high) customs duties.

Dick in Portugal was shocked one day to discover that the computer part friends sent him from the States, worth about $15, cost him $60 in customs duties. He later discovered that if the package had been marked "gift," he wouldn't have had the problem.

I don't know the rules for every country, but you may want to check the regulations where you are—or at least mark "gift" anyway. It can't hurt and may help get your package through.

Mailing/Secretarial Services

Professional mailing and secretarial services will collect your mail in the United States at their address or a post office box they provide, then forward it according to your instructions. Choose an independent secretarial service or one of the franchised services. First, though, make sure the personnel are familiar with overseas shipping. Ask if they have current clients for whom they perform this service.

Companies such as Pak Mail, Mail Boxes Etc., and others offer services throughout the United States and in many countries overseas. You rent a postal box at one of the locations and provide a deposit. Most also request that you leave a credit card number on file if you'll be overseas (I guess they just don't trust us runaways). Then, the company will follow your instructions for forwarding wherever you are.

Tip: Make sure that the forwarding service will accept parcels, UPS, and FedEx deliveries. The usual post office boxes won't accept parcels, but those connected with a secretarial service or location that has an actual street address can.

We found a Pak Mail center run by a husband-wife team who were already performing forwarding service for others overseas. We got the benefits of the professional franchise, a regular U.S. address, plus personalized service. We simply call John or Diane if we question whether something has arrived or if our mail has accumulated. We trust them to help decide whether or not it's worth sending a package.

After a trial-and-error period in which every bill we received was already overdue, we set up a three-times-a-month system in which mail was forwarded the fifth, fifteenth, and twenty-fifth of the month. That way we catch the first of the month's bills and get mail every ten days. Most of our bills now arrive with just enough time to pay them, so we're back in the good graces of our creditors.

If you use a postal box with forwarding, you'll pay a monthly fee for the box rental itself and a service fee based on the number of times per month you want your mail forwarded. You'll pay the postage costs, which will be deducted from the deposit you pay up front. As the deposit is depleted, replenish the account by sending a check or charging to your credit card. In our case, Diane puts a message into one of our mail packets that our postage account is running low, and we send her a check on our U.S. checking account.

SAMPLE FEES FOR MAIL FORWARDING SERVICE

Medium post office box: 1 year $72.00

Mail forwarding:	Once a month	$18 quarter	(plus actual postage)
	Twice a month	$24 quarter	(plus actual postage)
	Weekly	$36 quarter	(plus actual postage)
	Daily	$60 quarter	(plus actual postage)

The Drop Dead List

Almost as important as ensuring that important mail reaches you is ensuring that junk mail doesn't. Real junk mail won't be forwarded, but much of the first-class mail you receive consists of things you don't want to pay for overseas. I don't know about you, but I never read those beautiful, glossy—

and very heavy—annual reports. Even if you only have $10 in the stock fund, they send them to you. But it will cost you $40 in January to receive a plump package of them forwarded.

We called our stockbroker and requested that he take us off the mailing list and only send statements. We also told our mail forwarding service to hold any mail—even first class—that looks like advertising. Real estate agents, developers, automobile dealers, the new pizza place around the corner all rank among the guilty. We pick this mail up when we return to the States or have visitors from the States bring it just in case there's anything vital hidden there.

General Delivery/Poste Restante

If you're traveling from one city to another or don't have a permanent address yet, it's possible to have mail sent to a main post office overseas where it will be held for you. Ask your post office in the States which post offices at your destination handle general delivery mail and get their addresses and zip codes.

In Britain, France, Italy, and a multitude of European and Asian countries, your correspondents should address your mail to you, care of *poste restante*, city, country, and zip code. In Germany, the general delivery mail is called *postfach*. In some towns only the main post office will accept general delivery mail, so check before you have your correspondents send mail there.

When you arrive in the town, visit the post office you've selected to let them know that mail is expected. To pick up your mail, take your passport and another form of official (preferably with your photo) identification. You'll pay a small fee for the service based on the number of letters you receive.

Mail Drops
International Banks

Your bank overseas may be available as a reliable mail drop. International banks such as Barclays serve this purpose if you set up an account prior to leaving the States. Check with your current bank to see if they can recommend a bank in the country where you'll be.

American Express

American Express offers its cardholders a free mail drop service at offices throughout the world. Ask any American Express Travel agent for their booklet, *American Express Worldwide Traveler's Companion*. It lists American Express travel office locations in the United States and abroad and provides important phone numbers such as the Global Assist hotline and ATM locations where you can get cash using your American Express card in countries around the world.

American Express assumes no liability for your mail, but the company is reputable and takes pride in providing services worldwide. You may find it convenient and cost-effective, though you will need one of their cards to access the services. You'll pay an annual fee of $50 for the American Express card and are required to pay charges in full each month.

Post Office Boxes

You can rent a post office box through the postal service overseas or use a private secretarial service to collect your mail. If you travel often, this provides a stable home base for your mail. The only disadvantage is that you have to return to that post office box location often to find out if you have mail. If you're using that locale as your base overseas, this won't be a problem, but if your adventure entails traveling from place to place, this option won't work for you.

One important note: Mail to post office boxes will *not* be forwarded so make other arrangements when you plan to move on.

TELEPHONE CONNECTIONS

To make an international call from abroad you'll dial a code for the international operator, then the country code, the city code, and local number. You can do this from any regular phone. The trick is to find the most efficient and economical means of calling from abroad.

Foreign Calling Cards

In many countries you can purchase phone cards that are electronically set to provide a certain number of units for your phone calls. Many phones overseas, in fact, require a card.

Insert the card, make your call, and the amount of the call will automatically be deducted from the card. The number of units remaining shows on the phone display, so you can replace your card before it runs out of credit.

Phone cards are easy to locate. Airports usually have machines where you can purchase cards. In many countries, you'll find phone cards at the post office, tobacco shops, or other sundry shops in town.

Callback Services

For international calls at drastic discounts, Americans and other expats overseas swear by callback services. The name *callback* is literal, since you dial a special phone number provided by the company, let it ring once, then hang up (you're not charged for this call). The service immediately returns the call to you, with a message to dial the number you want to call, which is then put through.

You can use callback services if you're at a permanent location overseas, or for a slightly higher rate, you can order a "traveler number" or receive your callback call by name at a hotel or business.

International rates for callback services are considerably lower than most other means of calling. Best of all, callback rates usually apply twenty-four hours a day, so you can call when you want, not wait for special evening or holiday rates to call the kids or your stockbroker (who's on the golf course on Sundays in any case).

You can find a host of callback services advertised in papers such as the *New York Times* and *International Herald Tribune*. The biggest service, and the original, is named Kallback.

Contact Kallback toll-free in the United States at (800) 959-5255 or e-mail them at info@kallback.com. Their Web site includes reams of information on the service and how it works: www.kallback.com.

Long-Distance Calling Cards

Long-distance calling cards enable the traveler to dial a special number, which provides access to English-language operators to put calls through. We tried AT&T, so I'll use them as an example; however, Sprint, MCI, and others also offer calling cards. Investigate them as well, particularly if your home phone is already connected to one of these services.

With an international telephone card, you can use most public and private phones without needing coins. You'll dial an access number for the country you're calling, then the number plus the calling-card number, which serves as a security code.

If you already have a calling card, it's probably tied to a home or office phone number. You'll be able to use the card only if you maintain that home or business number while you're away. If you shut off your phone to close, rent, or sell your home, that card is no longer valid. To avoid this problem, request a "direct-billed" card from AT&T or other long-distance carrier. A direct-billed calling card is not associated with a specific area code; it's billed separately, so you don't need to have a U.S. phone number. Bill it to a major credit card, such as American Express, VISA, or MasterCard. You'll be paying in dollars, which may prove to be advantageous, and you'll only have to pay your credit card bill; no concern about a separate phone bill reaching you wherever you may be.

The AT&T calling card is free but you'll be billed at the AT&T rates. When using the card from a hotel room this will minimize surcharges that hotels typically tack on, but it's not the cheapest way to call internationally.

Additional services offered by AT&T include USA Direct, which connects you with an AT&T operator, so you don't have to worry about explaining a call in a foreign language. It works for any location in the States except Alaska from more than 120 countries and locations around the world.

AT&T's World Connect service works like USA Direct, but it functions from one foreign country to another foreign country. If you're in Italy, for example, and planning to go to Switzerland, you can call for hotel reservations. To use USA Direct or World Connect you'll pay a fee of $2.50 per connection, plus you pay for the first minute and each additional minute. The card can also be used within the United States for an eighty cents per minute surcharge.

You can sign up for different plans, including a so-called Military Calling Card, which is not reserved only for the military. Ask about it. If you intend to use the service, you pay a small additional fee and the rate is lowered. It's still a costly way to call, however.

A word of warning: The AT&T World Connect service costs a small fortune if you call from one country outside the United States to another outside the United States. I learned this the hard way with a $89 phone bill for one call from France to Portugal. It seems that AT&T routes the call from France to the United States, then the call is bounced back to Portugal. Admittedly, we talked for thirty minutes, but still almost $3 a minute was an utter shock. Use this only in emergencies.

For more information on the USA Direct/World Connect services, call the AT&T Customer Service Center at (800) 331-1140, ext. 746. For information on the direct-billed card, including countries where you can use it, call toll-free (800) 525-7955.

The Local Phone Overseas
If you settle into one location overseas, you can use your home phone for local and international calls. Check the rates to find the cheapest time to phone. You may discover that it's easier and relatively affordable to use your own phone on off-times for the occasional international call. However, if you make many calls, see the callback information above.

800 Numbers
Those 800 numbers we take for granted in the United States as being toll-free are not toll-free when you're calling from overseas. You must pay to get into the U.S. system. If using calling cards or other services, you'll still pay whatever charges apply to reach the United States.

Before you escape abroad, find out if any companies you deal with have alternatives to 800 numbers, which permit you to call collect. Our life insurance company, USAA, deals with military personnel overseas, so they provide a collect number to use if we ever have questions.

Specialized Communication Services

English Language/Translation

The AT&T Language Line provides professional interpreters in 140 languages, twenty-four hours a day, seven days a week. This makes it easy if you get in a real pickle overseas and need someone to help translate for you. There is a charge for the service, currently ranging from $5.25 to $7.25 per minute, depending on the language required. You receive personal interpretation and pay with your AT&T calling card or a major credit card. To see how the service works, try a free demonstration at (800) 821-9020.

The AT&T Language Line also provides written translation services with the charge based on the type of communication, whether personal or technical. For information, call (800) 648-0874, ext. 3.

AT&T Message Service

AT&T Message Service lets you record a one-minute message in your own voice and have the message delivered to virtually any phone in more than 200 countries. You can specify when you want your message delivered and even request a response.

I imagine this service could come in handy when you finally find a phone in Timbuktu but hear a busy signal just as the guide yells that the last llama is leaving with your luggage. In these dire straits you could call AT&T and forward your message. For information on the AT&T Message Service, call (800) 562-6275.

Telegrams/Mailgrams

Western Union offices in the United States send mailgrams throughout the world, which are delivered through the local telegraph or post office overseas. Messages will be phoned or delivered to you. Most of us have an image of telegrams as speedy. Claire in Portugal thought this was the case until it took three days for a telegram to reach her. Her comment was that she would have had a letter almost as fast.

If you want to send a telegram from overseas to someone in the United States, check your local phone book for Western Union locations near you.

The Internet

Connecting via the Internet creates a lifeline to family and friends, financial advisors, or anyone with an e-mail address anywhere in the world. It can even connect you to those who aren't on-line when you use your technoid cousin in Brooklyn as a conduit to share news with aunts and uncles.

E-mail is the next best thing to being there. In fact, it's such a valuable resource for every stage of the adventure, that the next chapter is devoted entirely to the Internet and ways to use it to keep in touch or otherwise find information that will enhance your trip.

17
The Internet Advantage

THE REAL VOYAGE OF DISCOVERY
CONSISTS, NOT IN SEEKING NEW LANDSCAPES,
BUT IN HAVING NEW EYES.
—Marcel Proust

If you're the least bit technically inclined, have some spare change for computer equipment, and plan to be located anywhere near phone connections, I highly recommend taking a notebook computer with an international fax/modem. This modern-day version of the pony express enables you to keep in touch with family and friends overseas. It also connects you with a world of information in the States and abroad.

E-Mail . . . The Next Best Thing to Being There

E-mail is not only less expensive than a phone call, it provides a powerful psychological link to family and friends. The Internet connection is instantaneous—or whenever your correspondent checks his or her e-mail. Spontaneity is another big plus. You can write ten times a day if you feel like it. You wouldn't make all those calls. My daughter knows more about what we're doing now than she ever did when we lived in the States.

You can e-mail any time, day or night, which with the time difference overseas is a wonderful advantage. After all, you can't exactly pick up the phone in Italy at 10 A.M. and call your friends in New York. Well, you can, but don't expect them to be happy about it when you wake them from that 4 A.M. dream.

They will, however, be thrilled by the fact that when they send you an e-mail after work in the States, they can have your response by the time they wake up the next morning. They'll think you're really on the ball. Just don't explain that though you sleep in and don't check e-mail until noon, it's still just 6 A.M. Eastern time.

These days you can even set up connections for voice communications. In the "old days" of computers, you needed to have specific equipment, but now your computer can be set to call anyone on a regular phone. I admit I'm not technically advanced enough to have tried it yet, but for those of you less intimidated by things electronic, it sounds like a wonderful solution to astronomical phone bills.

Trying to find the children at home at the same time we could get to a phone seemed almost impossible many times. We started using e-mail when we arrived in the Mediterranean, and found the pressure was off. One can send an e-mail any time and the receiver can receive at any time.
—Sue and Jim, worldwide cruisers

REACH A WORLDWIDE NETWORK OF INFORMATION

With a modem, your computer does much more than provide communication with your friends. You can access the Internet to find out the weather in the location you're thinking of visiting next, check your stocks, read the latest news in the States, and fill in the gaps from the magazines you're not getting. Yes, many magazines are actually on-line now, so you can avoid having them posted to you overseas. Just read the news on your computer.

Most major airlines have Web sites where you can access current information on flights and prices. Many of them use their Web sites to post last-minute international fares at discount prices.

You can find destination information galore on the Internet as well— maybe even the house you'll live in. I found a French *fermette* on a Web site, and it served well as our first base overseas until we got organized enough to find more permanent housing. You can check out countries and cities, train systems, museums, theaters, security, health needs, and much more.

CONNECT PERSONALLY WITH MESSAGE BOARDS

The message boards offered by some Internet providers enable you to connect or "meet" people with similar interests in the areas you are thinking of living or visiting. Not only is this interesting and informative, it can even lead to some surprising adventures. I "met" a woman who was in the midst of planning a move to Portugal. We talked on e-mail for several months about the joys and perils involved in our respective moves. Eventually, we wrote, spoke on the phone, and later visited each other. In fact, my husband

and I house-sat and dog-sat for Claire and Dick while they biked in Austria for several weeks. We made new friends and enjoyed living within a few miles of Algarve beaches, in a home complete with pool and maid—and I owed the experience all to the Internet message boards where we first met.

How to Network on the Net

Use on-line services to locate people living near the place you intend to visit. Then e-mail them for specific information. For example, AOL has a member list you can use to search by location. Type in the city, and the list will show you the e-mail addresses of members living there.

When I found the house on the Internet, I was unfamiliar with the specific area of the Loire Valley in France where it was located. I looked up members in cities in France nearby, then e-mailed a half dozen with questions. Three of the people e-mailed back and were very nice, providing the answers as well as they could. We even met one of them, a young French gendarme living just a half-hour drive from where we settled. The coffee and conversation were both interesting, and I got extra tips on connecting to the Internet from my new location.

Be very polite when you e-mail strangers. Remember, they are doing you a favor by replying. Excuse yourself for bothering them but explain that you are moving to their area, saw their name on an e-mail list as living there, and very much would like their help. Then have specific questions—three or four at the max.

Avoid taking undue advantage. You want personal feedback on information that would otherwise be difficult to obtain. Don't waste anyone's time by requesting basic travel information you could get from a book or travel agent. Save your questions for the nitty-gritty details that are important to you. If, for example, you can't go anywhere without taking a tennis racket, you might ask if there are good courts in the area. Or you could get information on the availability and average price for housing. This information isn't found in the usual guide books.

If the local language is not English, try to write in that language. If your skills aren't up to it, find a friend who will write the e-mail for you and translate the returning messages. Of course, if you find someone who's eager to chat with an American to practice their English, you're all set.

Equipment You'll Need

The Computer
The handiest computer to carry with you is a notebook style equipped with a dual voltage adapter that handles either 110 or 220 volts AC. These compact computers are lightweight for travel and fit just about anywhere, which is very useful if you're living in smaller accommodations overseas.

A regular desktop computer is less expensive than a notebook but bulkier. Some people who run away on a permanent basis purchase a desktop computer overseas. If you already have one and want to take it overseas, buy a transformer to convert the power. We did that with an IBM 486, which we now use as a backup computer and it works fine.

However, I still like my trusty notebook computer. Even if you have a permanent base overseas as we do, the notebook is a pick-up-and-go solution that enables you to travel and still take your e-mail with you. Once you're accustomed to communicating this way, it's hard to cut the (power) cord.

Don't Zap Your Computer!

The voltage used in North America, including the United States and Canada, is 110 volts. This is also used in Mexico, other areas of Central America, some parts of South America and parts of the Pacific. Everywhere else uses 220 volts, though some countries, such as Costa Rica, the Cayman Islands and others, use both. Most notebook computers make allowances for either but *beware of DC power in phone systems!* Some buildings have a central switchboard that uses DC power; usually this system requires you to go through the switchboard by dialing a number such as nine or eight for outside calls. These systems are much too high in electrical voltage for your modem. Do *not* connect your modem in these situations!

If you're concerned, a small testing device is currently on the market that purports to show whether or not a phone line is low voltage, and thus safe. They may have been perfected by the time of this printing; however, the one I purchased showed my home line, which I'd been using safely for ten years, to be dangerous. Since I knew it to be safe, I had no proof the tester would really determine the safety of a line overseas for better or worse. So I'm not sure I can recommend these devices. You may, however, find one that's been improved by the time you read this.

Adapter Plugs and Surge Protection

Once you've chosen the right computer, you'll need an adapter plug to fit the electrical system for whatever country you're in. For example, in most Western European countries, the plugs use two round pins, considerably different than the usual U.S. straight plug. You plug your computer into the adapter, then plug the adapter into the wall, or plug it into a surge suppressor, then the wall.

My surge suppressor is a small unit, only a few inches long, which fits conveniently into the notebook's travel bag. It won't survive a direct hit by lightning, I'm sure, but it does provide everyday protection from the surges and spikes that you can encounter overseas—or anywhere for that matter.

The Modem

The hardware your computer uses to connect to the phone line is called the *modem*. Some computers come with modems installed; otherwise, you can have one installed. Either way, be sure to buy a modem that's error correcting, as most new ones are. Overseas phone connections are, alas, not always as good as those in the States. You'll need the error correction to overcome the additional "noise" on the phone lines.

I purchased the top-of-the-line International Modem with my IBM laptop. It's worked beautifully. Many other modems can accomplish what you need; talk to a computer pro to see what they suggest.

The Phone Jack

The United States uses one type of phone plug, called a RJ11, which connects your phone, or in this case, your computer modem, to the wall outlet. In other countries, the phone plug is configured differently, so you'll need an adapter for the phone plug, just as you need an adapter for the electrical plug. You can find these at specialty suppliers, even on the Internet itself.

Walkabout Travel Gear is one retailer that has all the above equipment, complete with helpful personnel to answer your questions on using it. Call them toll-free at (800) 274-4277 or (800) 852-7085. They provide a Web page (www.walkabouttravelgear.com/wwelect.htm) that includes everything you ever wanted to know about electricity around the world, complete with a listing of which countries have which voltage and what adapter plugs work where. Indispensable!

Printers

In North America electricity is delivered at 110 volts and 60 cycles per second, or 60 hertz (Hz). In Europe it's delivered at 220 volts and 50 Hz. A transformer will adapt the voltage but not the cycles. A computer can handle the difference in cycles, but a printer can't. This is probably why you won't find a printer that works on both 110/220 voltage, as does a notebook computer. It wouldn't help.

If you want to print from your notebook computer in a country where the cycles per second, or hertz, differs, then buy a printer at your destination. I found mine in France, and though it was a bit nerve-racking setting it up with French instructions, having set up printers in the States enabled me to manage with intermediate French and a dictionary. Often, the information is printed in several languages, among them English, making the whole process even simpler.

Beware of Pseudo Experts

Today's small computers and the related communication equipment make running away easier than ever. Unfortunately for us escapees, it's not easy to purchase the right equipment for an overseas adventure. It took me months, lots of shoe leather, and a sore dialing finger to find out the above information. When you go to purchase a computer or modem in the States, most computer salespeople—and I use the term loosely—have never used a computer overseas, don't know anyone who has, and will still pretend to be all-knowing. So shop around and ask lots of questions. Take the above list with you and tell the salesperson that you intend to use the equipment for overseas connection. Then tell them again.

No Computer? Here's How to E-Mail Anyway

If you don't want to carry a computer on your trip but do want to take advantage of e-mail now and then, set up an account with a service provider, then beg or borrow a computer overseas. If you have friends overseas with a computer and modem, use it to connect to your own service provider by logging on as a guest.

In larger cities, cyber cafés offer computers by the hour. Some hotels have computer equipment in the lobby; for about $6 an hour on your credit card you can log on to pick up and send your e-mail. You may also be able to borrow accounts at universities or libraries to accomplish the same thing.

Ask your service provider how to access your account from another computer system. Then try the technique from a borrowed system in the States to ensure you know the basics before tackling it overseas.

Internet Service Providers

You'll need software to make your modem hardware work. The big providers in this arena have been narrowed down to America Online (AOL) and Microsoft Network, with AOL being far and away the largest. The large services have a long reach overseas, since they provide local phone numbers you can dial in many countries abroad. By taking a major Internet service provider and your e-mail address with you from the States, your correspondents will already know your address and you'll have access to member services as well as the Web.

Before signing up with an Internet provider, find out if they have connecting points (nodes in computerese) near where you'll be overseas. Small, local providers won't offer access around the world unless you dial into their phone lines long-distance, not exactly cost-efficient.

Ask what the service provider charges overseas. Even if they advertise a low price for unlimited service, their overseas providers under the same name are different, and you can be hit by costly surcharges. That may be OK for the occasional trip, but unacceptable if you're living in one location long-term.

Let me give an example: I signed up for AOL in the States and prepaid for unlimited service for a year on the special $17.95 per month deal. I left the United States and arrived in France to discover that I'm paying an additional $6 hourly surcharge here.

It hardly makes one feel good to pay an additional $45 to $50 every month for a service one thought was "unlimited." Learn from my mistake. If you're going to be settling somewhere abroad, ask before you leave the States what the policy and charges will be on overseas connections.

Local Internet Providers

You can use a local provider overseas to gain Internet access just as you would with any provider in the States. If you want to maintain your current service, perhaps to keep the on-line name that all your correspondents already know, get an Internet provider overseas for about $20 a month, then change your AOL or other account to a "bring your own provider" contract, which costs much less, usually about $9.95 month.

According to AOL instructions, you can access e-mail on AOL from another service provider by changing the network option at setup to TCP/IP. Sign on to your overseas Internet provider and minimize their screen; then launch America Online and sign on to it.

INTERNET SITES FOR EASIER ESCAPES

Find virtually any information required for running away in the virtual world of the Web. The list of helpful Internet sites extends ad infinitum, but here are a few relevant to adventures overseas.

Expatriate Groups
Association of Americans Resident Overseas (AARO)
members.aol.com/aaroparis/aarohome.htm
Founded in 1973, this nonprofit group represents U.S. citizens abroad. The site discusses the group's goals and achievements and offers membership and medical insurance overseas.

American Citizens Abroad (ACA)
iprolink.ch/aca/
This nonprofit association is dedicated to serving the interests of U.S. citizens abroad. The site links to information on moving overseas, travel advisories, information on finding jobs overseas, and more.

Embassy Page
www.embpage.org
Provides links to consulates and other overseas helps.

Escape Artist
www.EscapeArtist.com
Provides a large number of links related to overseas adventures, with many specifically directed toward retirement. Includes country information, embassy pages, and an expatriate chat room.

Expat Exchange
www.expatexchange.com/
A network of topics of interest to Americans overseas with links to job listings, employment services, tax, and financial information.

Expat Forum
www.expatforum.com
Provides services and information on living, working, traveling, and doing business overseas. Includes a message board, a bookstore for information on cultures and protocol, cost of living information, and Web links of interest to expats.

Intercultural Press
www.bookmasters.com/interclt.htm
Access this site to find a range of books related to living overseas.

Overseas Digest
overseasdigest.com/
Tips on security, emergency information, and legal assistance, among other topics for people heading overseas.

> *I found some great sites on the Internet with all sorts of help for*
> *people going overseas, or already there. We were making our plans then*
> *and it was exciting, like we were really going to do this!*
> —Maria Eugenia, 40, Caracas, Venezuela

Destination Information: General
American Express
www.americanexpress.com
Access to a travel and destination section that provides information on vacation specials, flights, car and hotel bookings, plus information on American Express business and financial services.

City.Net
www.city.net
This resource lets you search more than 5,000 destinations, providing fact sheets on cities in the United States and the world, with access to reservations, maps, and message boards.

CNN Travel
www.cnn.com/TRAVEL
Links to travel news and resources including currency, city guides, on-line reservations, and other travel-related happenings.

Destination Information: Country Specific
France
www.france.com
Information on French regions, history, culture, architecture, and activities. Also includes news (in French), on-line cafes, forums, classifieds. Offers French books if you're studying and want to practice.

Tennessee Bob's Famous French Links
www.utm.edu/departments/french/french.html
Francophile sites, books, art, music, history, language, and more, including access to numerous other sites for information on everyday life in France.

Mexico
mexico-travel.com/geninfo/index.html
Resource for information on Mexico sites.

Mexico
www.mexconnect.com/mex_/gmxhntl.html
For people moving to Mexico, here are hints from expat Scott Michael Long.

Language Training
If you're preparing for an adventure in a country where English isn't widely spoken, start learning the new language. Here are a few sites that will help.

Travlang's Foreign Language for Travelers
www.travlang.com/languages/
Options enable you to choose from multiple languages and categories, such as directions, times, dates, and so forth, to learn basic words. Links to other sites, such as dictionaries and pronunciation guides.

TECLA Lessons (Language Acquisition Center/The University of Texas at Arlington)
langlab.uta.edu/langpages/TECLA.html
An excellent source for reading exercises that consist of text written in everyday Spanish, with new vocabulary explained.

Bienvenue sur France Pratique
www.pratique.fr/sommaire.html
French language information for practice.

News
CNN Interactive
www.cnn.com
Current events, travel facts, weather, and features to keep you updated wherever you land.

International Herald Tribune
www.iht.com
Includes IHT special reports, features, classified ads and much more from the paper designed specifically for English speakers overseas.

Health and Overseas Advisories
Centers for Disease Control
www.cdc.gov/travel/travel.html
Comprehensive resource provides health recommendations based on geographical area and notes danger spots based on disease outbreaks.

U.S. State Department
www.stolaf.edu/network/travel-advisories.html
Provides travel warnings for Americans and consular information sheets. To request travel information by e-mail, send a message to travel-advisories-REQUEST@stolaf.edu

Bureau of Consular Affairs
travel.state.gov/index.html
Provides a range of information relevant to U.S. citizens abroad.

IAMAT (International Association for Medical Assistance to Travelers)
www.sentex.net/~iamat
Information on the service, which helps travelers locate English-speaking doctors and hospitals overseas.

Transportation
Airlines

Major airlines maintain Web sites with helpful information on flights, fares, and miscellaneous travel information. Many of these sites even let you book flights on-line. Start dreaming about your trip here:

Aeromexico	www.wotw.com/aeromexico
Air France/Air InterEurope	www.airfrance.fr/
American Airlines	www.americanair.com/
British Airways	www.british-airways.com/
Delta AirLines	www.delta-air.com/
Lufthansa Airlines	www.lufthansa.com/
Northwest Airlines	www.nwa.com/
KLM Royal Dutch Airlines	www.klm.nl/
Qantas	www.anzac.com/qantas/qantas.htm
Sabena	www.sabena.com/
Singapore Airlines	www.singaporeair.com/
Swissair	www.swissair.com/
Trans World Airlines	www.twa.com/
United Airlines	www.ual.com/

For more airline information:

Airline Links
www.redbay.com/sjipp/html/airline_links.html
This Web page provides links to virtually any major airline's Web site around the world. Just click and you can check on airlines from Aer Lingus to Air New Zealand.

Air Traveler's Handbook
www.cis.ohio-state.edu/hypertext/faq/
usenet/travel/air/handbook/top.html
This comprehensive site contains everything you want to know about finding inexpensive air fares.

Travelocity Web site from SABRE
www.travelocity.com
Request routing alternatives for U.S. and world sites, check fares, and follow links to airlines and destinations.

> *I frequently go two or three consecutive days without leaving the house; sometimes only to take out the garbage! Truth is, that I could entertain myself endlessly "surfing the net."*
> —Claire, 45, Algarve, Portugal

Rail
Eurail
www.eurail.com
Information includes guides, maps, and data on European train travel including rail pass information and on-line ordering.

Rail Pass Express
www.eurail.com/links.htm
Access site for Eurail passes, British Rail, Go Greece, the French TGV train system, and much more.

Rental Cars
Avis
www.avis.com
Information on reservations, rates, and locations worldwide.

Hertz
www.hertz.com
Access rates, reservations, and worldwide locations.

Housing
The Caretaker Gazette
www.angelfire.com/wa/caretaker
For a subscription of $24 a year you receive lists of homes wanting house sitters; mostly in the United States, but 10 percent or so are overseas.

Global Travel Apartments Comfort Zone
www.globaltrvlapt.com/
Provides lists of furnished accommodations available for extended stays; includes areas in North America, Europe, Asia, Australia, and Africa.

International Home Exchange Network
www.homexchange.com
Host travelers or exchange your home for another. Charges a fee to list your home or subscribe to the Web site.

Travel Exchange Club (merging with Stayfree Holiday Club)
www.travex.com/travex/home.html
Unlike some of the others, this club will list your home at no charge.

Moving Companies
Allied Van Lines
www.alliedvan.net/
Site helps you locate agents near you and provides tips on moving.

Vanpac International
www.vanpac.com/
Information on moving services, rates, and agents; plus links to related moving sites.

Tax and Financial Information
Banks of the World (IFBG Göttingen)
www.wiso.gwdg.de/ifbg/bank_2.html
Handy links to bank information in United States, Canada, Europe, and Asia and the locations of bank ATMs overseas.

MasterCard Currency Converter
www.oanda.com
Supplies tips on money exchange overseas with conversion tables, forecasts, and links to other financial sites.

Bloomberg Cross Currency Rates
www.bloomberg.com/markets/fxc.html
Chart of key currency rates in eleven major world currencies.

IFBG Göttingen
www.wiso.gwdg.de/lfbg/currency.html
Provides in-depth access to a huge variety of sites for information on currencies and currency exchange rates.

Cost of Living Comparisons
www.homefair.com/homefair/cmr/salcalc.html
Income calculator lets you compare the cost of living in various United States and international cities.

IRS Publication 54: Tax Guide for U.S. Citizens Abroad
www.irs.ustreas.gov/plain/forms_publs/pubs.html
Find the tax form needed for Americans residing abroad here.

Technical Information
Walkabout Travel Gear
www.walkabouttravelgear.com/wwelect.htm
This site is packed with essential information on international electricity, voltage, plug adapter, and modem requirements overseas. Provides the option to purchase the adapters, converters, and transformers needed for any area in the world.

Communication
TeleAdapt
www.teleadapt.com/
On-line catalog for products includes a Traveler Help Desk with tips on how to hook up overseas using phone adapters, plug adapters, modems, and more.

Work, Learn, or Volunteer
Club Med
www.clubmed.com
Trips for couples, singles, and families—and the second screen provides information on jobs available.

Earthwatch
gaia.earthwatch.org
Information on the Earthwatch program and upcoming expeditions.

Hospitality Net Virtual Job Exchange
www.hospitalitynet.nl/job
Lists jobs overseas for people in the hospitality industry.

Overseas Jobs
www.overseasjobs.com/
Provides hints on getting a job outside the United States.

Peace Corps
www.peacecorps.gov/
Information on volunteers, applications, countries, and opportunities available.

WW Teach
members.aol.com/wwteach/Teach.htm
Provides tips and links to information on international education and schools, including international teaching jobs.

18

Handling Finances from a Distance

THERE IS ONLY ONE SUCCESS—
TO BE ABLE TO SPEND YOUR LIFE
IN YOUR OWN WAY.
—Christopher Morley

When you run away from home, you won't want to run away from your money. If you do, give me a call, and I'll be glad to take custody of it.

However, you *will* need to simplify your affairs. It's difficult to relax with an aperitif on a sunny Mediterranean patio if you've just perused the *International Herald Tribune*'s financial pages and are now frantically trying to reach your broker to yell, "Sell!"

Once you've determined to run away, begin organizing your financial affairs so that they'll run on automatic pilot or the closest thing to it. This assumes your investments are not already so extensive as to require a cadre of trusted advisors (each of whom drives a Mercedes thanks to your business).

Start by reviewing your financial situation. If your money is spread far and wide, in individual stocks or other investments that require continual monitoring, appoint an administrator who can manage them for you when you're absent, or consolidate and simplify. Your choice depends on your specific financial situation, how long you'll be overseas, and your willingness to entrust financial affairs to someone else.

Our decision was to simplify, for one important reason: Once out of the rat race, we didn't want complications with our finances. We weren't running away to spend the time concerned about market timing or wondering where our next baguette would come from if the stock market went south.

We consolidated investments with one broker who happens to also be a friend we trust. We closed one of our two U.S. checking accounts, but kept one that we use for bills that must be paid in dollars, such as our credit card payments and health insurance. The U.S. checking account is refreshed monthly, thanks to Social Security and the rental income from our house in the States, so that account funds daily living expenses like groceries, gasoline, and entertainment. We access it overseas through automatic teller machines. We slide in the U.S. bank card and out pops local currency at an excellent exchange rate.

We also opened an overseas checking account through a French bank, before we left the United States. We use the French checking account for expenses to be paid in francs, such as utilities. It's easy to open checking accounts in most countries, and expats who are overseas for more than a few months need them to pay bills in the foreign currency.

We've simplified to the point that we pay our U.S. bills three mornings a month (the three mornings we receive our forwarded mail with the bills in them!).

PUTTING INVESTMENTS ON AUTOMATIC PILOT

Having investments that don't require continuous oversight makes your adventure easier. The downside of this is that it limits your choices to investments that stay on an even keel. You may have to sell individual stocks or trust them to continue safely on track. You could probably leave Treasury bonds, or even Coca-Cola stock, and count on your money being around when you return. You could choose many other investments as well—but that hot little software stock that could turn on a dime is not one of them.

One way to simplify is to decide on a solid mix of stock, bond, and money market funds. Funds are already professionally managed, so from your point of view, they pretty much run themselves. Automatic reinvestment of dividends keeps your money earning while you're away, or you can have your broker deposit any interest or dividends in a money market fund, which you can draw from for living expenses.

When we simplified, we reviewed our finances with our friend the broker and ditched a few investments that were too dicey to allow for sound sleep in France. We also reviewed our balance of investments and selected a safer course rather than the more aggressive one.

PAYING BILLS LONG-DISTANCE

Arrange to keep funds available in an account that you can access wherever you'll be for cash. For U.S. bills, arrange to pay them yourself from overseas or have your banker or broker set up a program of automatic payments for bills such as mortgage or insurance, ensuring those bills are paid on time. The advantage of automatic payment is that they're paid no matter how long it takes for you and your mail to connect. When bills are forwarded, they can be overdue even before you receive them. Don't take a chance on losing your health insurance because you missed a payment.

If you want to mail the checks yourself, mark the due dates for mortgage, insurance, credit card, and other creditors on a small pocket calendar. Even if you haven't received the actual bill yet, make the payment. Since you won't be enclosing a billing stub, remember to write your account number on the check—a good habit in any case.

Take a supply of envelopes and deposit slips for your bank with you overseas. If you receive any checks for deposit, you can simply mail them in. The bank will mail you a receipt.

If you're traveling, sailing, or otherwise unable to write the checks and lick the stamps yourself, here are some additional ways to handle financial details from overseas.

Family Matters

Do you have a relative or close friend who is willing, able, and trustworthy enough to handle your financial affairs while you're gone? In an ideal world, you will. But this isn't an ideal world, and not many of us would want to take the responsibility for another's hard-earned nest egg. (Well, some people would, but those are the ones who plan to run away too—with your money!) The amount of time you'll be away makes a difference. Your brother may not mind handling your bills for three months, but two years may be pushing it.

Whomever you choose, fund a separate checking account with just enough money to pay expenses while you're gone, then provide authorization for the person to write checks on that account only. Your representative will have the ability to pay bills, but if that person suddenly loses at the track he won't be tempted to go through your entire life's savings.

Before you go, discuss how the person should handle emergencies themselves and when they should contact you.

Before we took off on this venture we found someone we trusted implicitly who handled our mail, responded to any necessary inquiries, and paid all our bills. This made our exit much easier and smoother than it might otherwise have been. We did also try to sell most of our personal effects and simplify our finances.
—Sue and Jim, worldwide cruisers

Professional Administration

If your portfolio is large (oh, to be so fortunate) or if it's extremely complicated, you may need to hire professionals to manage your financial affairs while you're gone. Your accountant or lawyer may be willing to handle everyday tasks, since they're already familiar with your finances. One or the other may agree to have their office accept bills, pay them, and manage financial situations as they occur. As with friends or relatives, you can arrange the checking account so your accountant or lawyer can write checks for you.

Decide in advance when your administrators should use their own judgment about expenses, when they should contact you, and what they should do if you can't be reached.

A Note about Power of Attorney

If you choose a friend, relative, or professional to administrate your funds, supply them with power of attorney. The limited power of attorney gives your representative specific control over certain of your financial affairs, for example, paying your bills. A general power of attorney would give the person complete control. Your attorney can arrange either type, but be sure you know which rights you are transferring before you sign anything. Be sure you trust that person to whatever extent you provide the power. Unless she's a trusted cousin, it might not be the smartest idea to provide power to buy and sell stocks to a broker who gets a commission every time she does so.

KEEPING YOURSELF IN CASH

Cash Exchange

Obtain a small amount of your destination's currency at an exchange desk at the international airport when you depart. Have enough to handle the immediate arrival expenses of taxis, subways, or a quick lunch. When you need to change more money, use your bank card at an automatic teller machine if possible; if not, find a large bank for the exchange. Either one of these options will offer a better rate of exchange than most street-side currency exchange services found in tourist areas.

Automatic Teller Machines

Automatic teller machines are the fastest, easiest, and most affordable way to access your money in the form of the local currency.

Remember two things and you should have no problems: First, always use your ATM card at a bank affiliated with your card network, for example, Cirrus, which is common overseas. Ask your bank for a list of locations overseas where your card will be accepted. For Cirrus cards, you can find the location of any of their 300,000 ATMs in ninety-four countries worldwide by calling (800) 424-7787.

Second, check that your code is acceptable for use overseas, which usually means that it must have only four digits. If yours has five, change it before you leave. Then test it at an ATM before taking it overseas. If you're part of a couple, you should each take a card. You'll be able to access cash individually (but keep track!), and you'll have a backup in case one card becomes damaged. If you're traveling alone, you can also take two cards, in case one becomes damaged. Just ask your bank for an extra.

You shouldn't have problems understanding foreign ATM machines. They offer a choice of languages, and English is usually one of them. Like most Americans overseas, we withdraw money regularly from our U.S. checking account for living expenses near our European base and when traveling. We've accessed Italian lira, British pounds, Portuguese escudos, and Spanish pesetas with equal ease.

I have two accounts, one in the States, one in France.
I use the ATM to get francs for spending money or I deposit the
francs to plump up the French checking account.
—Frances, 57, Antibes, France

Traveler's Checks

When you're traveling or first arrive overseas, traveler's checks provide safety and peace of mind. They can be cashed in any large bank, exchange offices, large shops, hotels, or restaurants. Don't count on them, however, for small restaurants or shops. Keep some cash available.

Travelers' checks are available in U.S. dollars or foreign currency. Check the exchange rate before you leave, to see which would offer a better value.

One expat discovered that his American Express traveler's checks were treated as cash, making transaction fees lower than wiring money, so he uses them to convert money from dollars to foreign currency and vice versa. Since he works overseas and is paid in foreign currency, he uses this technique to send money back to his U.S. accounts, though the technique works in reverse as well.

> *My practical trick to transfer money either way (from or to dollars) is to use traveler's checks. To go from dollars to foreign currency, buy dollar traveler's checks with a personal check. I use the American Express office [Author's note: This assumes you have a Gold Card]. A deposit in traveler's checks is normally treated as cash, so transaction fees are low and the exchange rate's better. Going the other way, buy traveler's checks overseas in dollars, restrictively endorse them as "for deposit only," and mail to your bank in the States.*
> —Doug, 43, Basel, Switzerland

Cash Advances

You can get cash advances on your major credit card through most banks that handle the cards, but this can be an expensive way to finance your trip. Credit card cash advances incur a higher interest rate. If you take an advance on your card and don't pay it immediately, which is likely when you're traveling, the interest charges start to accrue immediately.

The only way to avoid this is to "prepay" the card so you have cash built up to cover the advance or, the minute you take an advance, send a check to cover it. But if you had the money in the first place, why use the cash advance? My advice is to simply use the ATM or other sources for normal travel cash. Save the advances on your credit card for a serious emergency.

Emergency Cash from Home

You're in Bangkok and home's Boston. You're totally out of funds, and one ATM card cracked in half. The extra card just became dinner for the ATM machine. You're desperate. How to get funds?

MoneyGram. You can receive up to $20,000 in a day, in two transactions of $10,000 each, within minutes via computerized money transfer. Due to the speed, this method is the most accommodating to your travel schedule as long as you can get to one of their overseas offices to pick up the check. No waiting in one place for two or three business days for the money to come through. The fee is about $150 for $5,000 sent, but it will vary depending on the country and the dollar amount requested. For information, call (800) 926-9400.

Western Union. This is the old standby for wiring cash. In an emergency, you can have cash sent by using your Visa or MasterCard, or else someone at home can take cash or a certified check to a Western Union office. The cash can be picked up or delivered to you. The fee is about $68 per $1000 sent, but it varies based on amount requested and destination. For information, call (800) 325-6000.

Bank Wire Transfers. Transfer funds from your bank or stockbroker in the States to a bank account overseas. You'll need a string of information and numbers, which your overseas bank will give you. You can then provide this data to the stateside financial institution doing the transfer. The wire transfer itself doesn't take long, but allow a day or two for administration and time zone differences. You'll pay a fee for the service.

Consulate. In a real emergency, U.S. citizens can contact the U.S. consulate and arrange for funds to be sent by a bank or relatives via the Department of State's Overseas Citizen's Services. The money can then be picked up at the consulate overseas.

SOCIAL SECURITY, PENSIONS, AND OTHER REGULAR DEPOSITS

For safety, have your Social Security check deposited directly into your bank account in the States. Choose the account that is tied to your bank's automatic withdrawal card. Then you can simply withdraw cash as you need it in any currency and at very favorable bank exchange rates.

Do the same with your pension or other income checks.

THE TAX MAN COMETH . . . EVEN OVERSEAS

April 15 occurs inside and outside the United States, so you'll still have to file a tax return. However, if you're living outside the country on April 15 (or traveling for fourteen continuous days, including April 15) you're allowed an automatic two-month extension for filing. You'll need to attach a statement to this effect to your return. The catch-22 is that, if you owe taxes and they're not paid as of April 15, you'll incur interest charges.

For federal tax forms abroad, contact the U.S. embassy. The embassy does not supply state forms. Have your accountant handle it or ask someone in that state to send the correct forms to you.

For more information on extensions and other tax regulations for people living abroad, order the related publications by calling (800) TAX FORM (829-3676). Some publications of particular interest include #54, *Tax Guide for U.S. Citizens and Resident Aliens Abroad;* #776, *Overseas Filers of Form 1040;* #901, *U.S. Tax Treaties;* and #593, *Highlights for U.S. Citizens and Resident Aliens Abroad.* These are just a few of the topics that pertain directly to overseas residents, but there are other materials. An information booklet lists all the publications currently available.

If you have questions abroad, embassies can direct you to an IRS representative. The larger embassies even have IRS representatives assigned to them.

Uncle Sam's $70,000 "Gift"

If you live and work overseas, you may be eligible for an exclusion of up to $70,000 from your earned overseas income from wages, salaries, or professional fees, and even some housing amounts, provided you meet the length of stay guidelines. It sounds too good to be true, but the U.S. government assumes that if you work overseas you're not enjoying the U.S. benefits, so they allow you to exclude paying taxes on some earnings. The $70,000 figure is currently being debated for possible changes. For more information, order the current IRS publication #514, *Foreign Tax Credit for Individuals*.

Due to the complications involved in IRS regulations, talk to your tax advisor on how IRS regulations will affect your finances. Jane Bruno, a tax consultant who lived and worked in Germany, South Africa, and the United States, advises that

> foreign taxes on earned and unearned income can be an unpleasant surprise for those who haven't done their homework. Prepare tax estimates on projected income for a year both in the U.S. and in the foreign country to be sure the total tax picture makes financial sense.

We didn't do this, but sad to say, we're not in a big tax bracket and weren't intending to work overseas. However, we did talk to our accountant about various implications of living overseas. If you're concerned about the bottom line, take Jane's suggestion. If it's too difficult for you to do the projections, consult an expert in foreign taxes.

Better to investigate before your investments go traveling in a direction you don't want them to go.

19

Safeguarding Your Health Overseas

HE WHO HAS GOOD HEALTH IS YOUNG.

—H. G. Bohn

One year, just before leaving for Mexico for a short trip, I met with a client who had the flu. Three days later I was running a 103-degree fever, shivering uncontrollably, and wondering if my body should be buried in Mexico or shipped home. Is this any way to have fun overseas? No, but I lived to tell the tale and discovered that, while being sick away from home isn't any more fun than being sick in the States, it is possible to get care—and often very good care.

However, if you run away in midlife, you need to be assured that, should something happen to your health that require more than gallons of orange juice and aspirin, you will have the resources to be cared for properly. This is entirely possible overseas and shouldn't deter you from having this adventure.

The expats I talked with were all happy with their health care. Either they chose their location well or found a network of good health-care providers. I think it's a combination.

When Andrew had the car accident they helicoptered him
to an excellent hospital 23 kilometers away. Of course, the car
was a mess; I took the taxi but it was outrageously expensive so
our friends rallied 'round and took me back and forth.
—Christine, 54, Loire Valley, France

DOES YOUR HEALTH INSURANCE TRAVEL?

Aspirin and cough medicine are minor expenses that you can survive. You must protect yourself and your savings from the major expenses that are normally covered by medical/surgical insurance.

You probably already have health insurance, but your current coverage may not extend overseas. Don't just assume that it does. Ask your insurance carrier exactly what your health insurance covers when you're out of the country. Ask if it makes a difference *how long* you're out of the country as well. They may cover you for an emergency on a vacation but not if you're gone for months.

In some cases, the insurance will not provide any coverage at all. In some situations, it will cover you for emergencies, but you must pay the expenses out-of-pocket first, then be reimbursed by the insurer later; more often than not, a U.S. insurer will not pay foreign hospitals directly, and you will be required to have the bills translated from a foreign language and convert the currency amounts to dollars.

Check your specific insurance carrier before going overseas since major insurance companies and HMOs all differ in their coverage, sometimes even within the same company, depending on the state you live in or the group with which you're associated.

If you want a sabbatical overseas but plan to return to your job, investigate taking a leave of absence, maintaining your status as an employee in order to keep your health insurance in force under the group policy. You will probably have to pay the premiums yourself, but they'll be lower than paying for individual coverage.

Emergency Medical Evacuation

Emergency medical evacuation is the term for the transportation you would need, by air or ground transportation, if you had a medical emergency while in a remote area. You may not need this coverage if you intend to be in a cosmopolitan area with excellent medical services. But if you're planning a trip to the Himalayas or the Sahara desert, consider it. If you ever did require emergency medical evacuation from that oasis in the desert, the cost could reach tens of thousands of dollars.

> *I needed an electroconversion or "shock" to put my heart back into proper rhythm. It's an outpatient procedure in the States but when I told the cardiologist here, he was the one shocked. He couldn't believe that U.S. hospitals wouldn't keep the patient to prepare properly and then monitor afterwards. So I received excellent care. I was worried it would cost more due to the hospitalization, but the fee ended up being less than the outpatient treatment would have been back in the States.*
>
> —John, 62, Loire Valley, France

Overseas Coverage

Below is a general list of the coverage offered overseas by some of the major U.S. insurance providers. This is by no means comprehensive. In any case, it's essential to check the coverage on your own health insurance policy before leaving. These companies have numerous groups and may vary in coverage or may change their policies and procedures in the time it takes to plan your adventure.

Aetna. No coverage outside the United States.

Allstate. No coverage outside the United States.

Blue Cross/Blue Shield. Major medical group plans will reimburse for health care abroad if all documentation is provided in English, with payment records in dollars. Does not cover emergency medical evacuation. HMO participants have the same coverage but must contact their primary-care physicians before treatment.

Note: Blue Cross/Blue Shield has begun promoting a new European benefits program that is available overseas and includes medical evacuation and repatriation. See "Long Term Health Coverage" below.

Kaiser Permanente. Fully covers care in emergencies. Requires proof of payment for reimbursement. Checkups, dental care, and emergency medical evacuation are not covered.

Metlife. Covers emergencies only.

Nationwide. Reimburses costs if documents are in English and payments are converted to dollars. Emergency medical evacuation varies depending on the policy.

If your insurance does cover you overseas, add insurance reimbursement forms to your packing list. You can fill them out and mail them to the States from wherever you are.

Once more, please check your specific insurer regarding the policy you hold before leaving. Rules change, and your health insurance is too important to leave to chance.

COBRA Coverage

If you're leaving a job, you may be eligible to purchase insurance coverage at your group rate for up to eighteen months and later convert it to an individual policy. This solution will provide coverage less expensively and is an ideal solution if you plan to be gone eighteen months or less and will return to the states to continue working. It would also come in handy if you're 63½ and plan to return at 65 to use Medicare coverage.

MEDICARE ALERT!

Medicare will not cover Americans overseas, except, in limited circumstances, in Canada and Mexico. If you must count on Medicare, plan your adventure before you turn sixty-five, then return to take advantage of its benefits. Or, if your budget allows, you can buy private coverage for use overseas, then use Medicare when you later return to the States. Contact the American Association of Retired Persons for information about foreign medical care coverage that offers Medicare supplement plans.

I'm going to live longer here.
—Bill, 62, Saint Julien, France

Overseas Insurance Specialists

If your current U.S. health insurance does not provide overseas coverage, investigate companies that specialize in expatriate coverage. Policies that eliminate U.S. coverage carry a much lower premium—often it's just a third the cost—since the insurers avoid dealing with the high medical and liability costs of the U.S. health-care system.

Several older expats cut their costs by maintaining a high deductible on their overseas policies so that they're covered for a major emergency, but they pay for regular doctor and dentist visits themselves, or as one told me, "I can afford the $17 doctor appointment; it's the open heart surgery I wouldn't want to pay for."

TRAVEL/MEDICAL ASSISTANCE PROGRAMS

You'll see many ads for travel health insurance, but travel insurance only covers trips of two weeks up to seventy days. This short-term coverage is intended for vacationers, not people wanting to experience living overseas, so don't confuse it with regular health insurance.

Just as flight insurance is more expensive than regular life insurance, travel health coverage is much more expensive than regular health insurance. However, you'll find some information below so you will be aware of what's available. Such insurance may serve as a stopgap measure or work for your exploratory trips before going overseas long-term.

Typically, short-term travel insurance offers services such as trip cancellation, delay, emergency medical assistance, medical evacuation, and emergency consultation by phone or assistance in reaching the nearest hospital or English-speaking physician. These policies do not necessarily provide health insurance coverage itself, though some may.

Firms offering trip coverage include

Access America, 6600 W. Broad St., Richmond, VA 23230; (800) 284-8300. Policies are for short trips, up to fifteen days.

International Association for Medical Assistance to Travelers (IAMAT), 417 Center St., Lewiston, NY 14092; (716) 754-4883. Provides a worldwide directory of English-speaking physicians who have been screened for education and who charge reasonable fees. The service is for travelers only, not for people living overseas. However, nothing prevents you from joining IAMAT for your exploratory trips. Membership is free, though a tax-deductible donation is suggested. You'll receive a membership card and a world directory of physicians in 125 countries who speak English. Other benefits include a traveler's clinical record to provide your medical history and immunization record, a world immunization chart, malaria risk chart, and schistosomiasis risk chart.

International SOS Assistance, PO Box 11568, Philadelphia, PA 19116; (800) 523-8662. Provides emergency evaluation services, worldwide medical referrals, and optional medical insurance for up to fourteen days.

Medex, Timonium Corporate Center, 9515 Deereco Road, 4th Floor, Timonium, MD 21093; (800) 537-2029 or (410) 453-6300; e-mail: medex-asst@aol.com. Medical assistance services are available ranging from one day to one year. This company also offers a renewable policy for residence abroad that covers emergency medical evacuation and services in locating and negotiating medical care, emergency medical evacuation, or repatriation of remains. Also sells specialized medical kits for travelers to countries where sterile supplies are not readily available.

Travel Assistance International, 1133 15th St. NW, Suite 400, Washington, DC 20005-2710; (800) 821-2828. Offers medical assistance services and communication and limited emergency medical evacuation.

TravMed International Traveler's Assistance Association, 1765 Business Center Drive, Suite 100, Reston, VA 20190; (800) 732-5309. Offers twenty-four-hour access to Medex hotline, emergency evacuation, and dental coverage. Covers up to seventy days; however, their sister company, Wallach, handles longer trips (see below).

Wallach & Company (HealthCare Abroad/MedHelp Worldwide/HealthCare Global), 107 West Federal Street, PO Box 480, Middleburg, VA 20118; (800) 237-6615. This company offers several different options from traveler's insurance to comprehensive medical coverage overseas, including emergency medical evacuation services worldwide. Policies cover six months to twelve months but you're allowed two renewals for a minimum three months to another twelve months (three years maximum). Long-term coverage up to the age of seventy-six. For ages seventy-six to eighty-four, ask about their HealthCare Global policy.

> *I have a modest private health policy in England, but don't assume your coverage will continue indefinitely until you check it carefully. I know one woman whose husband reached his sixty-fifth birthday when he was in the hospital and the policy canceled right in the middle of it!*
> —Judy, 62, Athens, Greece

Long-Term Health Coverage Overseas

You'll need health insurance overseas for long-term coverage (a) if you intend to stay overseas more than the fifteen to seventy days covered by most travelers' policies, (b) your own U.S. policy won't cover you overseas, or (c) you want less-expensive coverage. Health insurance is more affordable when you purchase it for use overseas through specialized companies that don't have to deal with the high expense of the U.S. health-care system. If your policy is cost prohibitive in the United States, that's reason alone to run away from home.

When choosing an insurer, take the time to understand what the plan covers. Some health insurance plans will pay for emergency medical evacuation, for example. Others will arrange it for you, but you pay for it separately.

Beware preexisting condition exclusions. If you're been treated for a health problem recently, you may not be covered immediately for that condition. The usual waiting period seems to be two years. (One exception is International SOS Assistance's evacuation coverage, which has no such exclusion; however, that is simply short-term coverage.)

Here are a few of the larger companies that provide health insurance coverage to American expatriates:

BUPA International, Russell Mews, Brighton, Great Britain BN7 2NR, United Kingdom; telephone (UK) 44 1273 208 181; fax (UK) 44 1273 866 583. BUPA is one of the largest overseas health-care insurers specializing in health insurance for individuals and their families who live and work outside their home country.

ExpaCare Insurance Services, Dukes Court, Duke Street, Woking, Surrey GU21 5XB, England; telephone (UK) 44 1483 717 800; fax (UK) 44 1483 776 620. Offers a StandardCare Plan for hospitalization and emergency transport and a more comprehensive SpecialCare Plan for outpatient and other costs. Works with International SOS to provide twenty-four-hour-a-day multilingual assistance.

International Health Insurance Danmark a/s, 64a Athol Street, Douglas, Isle of Man, British Isles, IM1 1JE; telephone (UK) 44 1624 677 412. Owned by Denmark's largest national health insurance company, International Health Insurance insures expats of all nationalities in more than 140 countries. They offer several choices of health plans to cover hospitals, doctors, medicine, and ambulance transport. Dental, spectacles/contact lens coverage, and medical evacuation insurance are also available.

Lloyds Expatriate Protection Plans, U.S. toll-free number (800) 399-3904; Web site: www.artitude.com/costa. England's oldest insurance syndicate offers health insurance specifically designed for people living outside the country for which they hold a passport. Coverage for medical expenses is based on the area of the world where you intend to use it. People to age seventy-five are eligible.

PPP International Health Plan, Phillips House, Crescent Road, Tunbridge Wells, Kent, TN1 2PL; telephone (UK) 44 1892 512 345; fax (UK) 44 1892 515 143. One of the United Kingdom's leading medical insurance companies with over two million members. The International Division specializes in insurance for people working or living overseas; includes full-refund emergency evacuation service.

Blue Cross and Blue Shield of Western Europe, 59, rue de Châteaudun, 75009, Paris, France; telephone (France) (33) 1 42 81 98 76; fax (33) 1 42 81 99 03. Offers American style health insurance plans that may be costlier than some European plans, but if you already have a current Blue Cross insurance plan in the States, you can transfer into the Western Europe plan without a physical exam and transfer back to the U.S. plan on your return—with no preexisting condition exclusion period. Also, this plan will provide direct billing and advice in English.

Reciprocal Health Agreements

Some health insurance companies have set up reciprocal agreements, enabling you to transfer coverage from a company in the States to another company overseas. The benefit is that you can maintain your policy and avoid preexisting condition exclusions. For example, U.S. Blue Cross and Blue Shield can be transferred to a Blue Cross Blue Shield Western Europe policy (mentioned above) or to the Voluntary Health Insurance Company if you'll be living in Ireland. Ask your insurer if the company has any such reciprocal agreements. They're rare but it won't hurt to ask.

At ages 65 and 70 we have to be realistic but we enjoy good health.
We both walk every day and I try to swim most every day and am only
lax about bicycling due to time. We have accident insurance here, but
our major health insurance is for the States. Much as we like it here,
it doesn't make sense for us to retire completely in Venezuela.
—Susan, 65, Caracas, Venezuela

SELF-INSURANCE

Some people who can't get affordable health coverage in the States self-insure by setting aside money to cover medical expenses in a less-expensive country. Many choose to pay most medical bills but have insurance with a high deductible. Their savings wouldn't pay for open-heart surgery, but it does cover basic care and enables them to purchase insurance with a higher deductible and therefore lower monthly payments.

In many countries overseas, medical care is much less expensive than in the States, so some expats take a calculated risk. They "self-insure" by paying their own health expenses overseas and assume they will return to the States in case of serious situations to use Medicare or private insurance they have there. I don't recommend this route, since I want the peace of mind gained by knowing that emergencies and major medical costs would be covered.

Our health insurance has a high deductible, so we pay most doctor and dentist visits ourselves. The consolation is that health services where we live are excellent but much less costly than we were accustomed to. We were happily shocked to discover that the recommended French physician who spent nearly an hour with my husband charged him $17. A two-hour consultation with the head of the cardiology department and one of his interns cost just $60.

HEALTH CARE OVERSEAS

If you reside in another country, even as a U.S. citizen, you can sometimes participate in that country's health-care system. Residents of Ireland, whether or not they're Irish citizens, get free outpatient services, free care in public hospitals, and refunds on prescriptions over a certain price. People retiring as residents of Mexico can participate in the Mexican National Health Insurance Plan, which costs just $240 year—including dental and eye care. In many countries, if you work within the borders, you will pay into that country's social security system and therefore be covered for health care.

We pay about $28 for a visit to a doctor's office, double
that for a house call . . . but when was the last time you heard
about that! Our doctor speaks good English, too.
—Anne, 61, Albufeira, Portugal

Healthy Planning Steps

Start your adventure by planning for health care and you'll be prepared when you first arrive overseas or suddenly need care.

Medical
- Tell your physician about your plans to be overseas long-term and have any checkups a few months before leaving, so you can get a clean bill of health or handle any potential problems.
- Have the required immunizations and collect any special records you need to take with you to explain a medical condition and medications, for example, a copy of your EKG, blood type, X rays, or other records.
- If you have a serious condition, such as diabetes or a heart problem, that should be monitored regularly, get recommendations of specialists who practice at your destination before leaving. As soon as you arrive, contact the physician and have a get-acquainted checkup. You'll then have a source for your prescriptions or emergency consultations.
- Medic Alert bracelets or necklaces notify medical personnel that you have a problem, such as allergy, epilepsy, a rare blood group, or heart condition. The jewelry item is engraved with your member number and the twenty-four-hour Medic Alert phone number, which health-care workers can call to get details on your condition. For information on ordering, call Medic Alert at (800) 432-5378.

Immunizations
- Verify that your immunizations are current for the normal communicable diseases such as measles or tetanus.
- Check to see if you need any special immunizations for your destination. Western Europe requires the normal precautions of the United States. Less-developed areas of the world may require an international certificate of vaccinations against yellow fever and cholera. Hepatitis vaccinations are available and recommended in many parts of the world. Typhoid vaccinations, malaria medication, or other preventative measures are not usually required, but may be recommended for high-risk areas.
- Find out the exact requirements for your destination by contacting your local or state health department or physician; some physicians specialize in travel immunology and stay current on needs for foreign countries.
- The U.S. Public Health Service provides recommendations on inoculations for travel throughout the world in *Health Information for International Travel*, which is $5 from the U.S. Government Printing Office, Washington, DC 20402-9325. The Centers for Disease Control in Atlanta provides information on inoculations needed for destinations overseas at (404) 639-2572 or through their fax line at (888) 232-3299.

- If visiting countries with serious diseases, start immunizations or medications far in advance of departure. Some may cause reactions and you'll want to travel healthy.
- Have vaccinations recorded on World Health Organization approved forms and keep them with your passport.

Prescriptions

- If you take a prescription medication regularly, pack enough to last several months, so you have time to get settled overseas before needing more.
- *Always* keep medicines in their original prescription containers—not pill cases—so you can show the labels to doctors, pharmacists, or customs personnel if necessary.
- Prescriptions written by your doctor in the States will *not* be honored overseas, but have your doctor write one anyway, using the drug's generic name. Brand names vary widely from country to country but the generic should be readable by your doctor or pharmacist overseas in case of questions.
- Some drugs that can only be purchased by prescription in the States can be bought over-the-counter in foreign countries or vice versa.
- Drug laws are stricter in many countries. If you're in doubt about whether a medication is legally permitted, carry a letter from your physician. The same goes for needles and syringes. If you need regular injections, for diabetes, for example, take a letter from your physician confirming the medical necessity.

FINDING GOOD HEALTH CARE OVERSEAS

What if you become ill overseas? Don't panic over the mere thought. Many doctors and hospitals overseas are not only available but offer excellent care. Go prepared to find the best medical services you can.

Take a list of medical doctors who speak English. Sometimes you can accomplish this by simple word-of-mouth. It turned out that my dentist in Atlanta, a true francophile, had a French dentist friend. Though that dentist was in Paris, two-hours away, having a name before I arrived was at least comforting. As it turned out, I found two excellent French dentists just a few kilometers away through expats we met in town.

Medical specialists can refer you to other specialists throughout the world. My husband's cardiologist provided names of three cardiac specialists, one of whom spoke some English, within thirty minutes of our location in the French countryside. He didn't know them personally, but used the authoritative reference called the *Directory of Medical Specialists*. Your physician should have it. If not, check the library.

You can also write the Office of Overseas Citizens Services, Room 4811, 2201 C Street NW, Washington, DC 20520. Specify which country you're going to and they can provide names of medical providers in that area.

Once you've actually settled into life overseas, find good doctors, dentists, and hospitals by asking the nearest U.S. Embassy or consulate, other expats, your neighbors, or a pharmacist. Look for a university-affiliated teaching hospital in a major city.

A Real Emergency
Let's say you just arrived. What do you do if you break a leg as you trip over the baggage cart in the airport?

Here are a few forms of emergency assistance to remember:

The U.S. Embassy or consulate will help you find medical assistance and, at your request, inform family and friends.

International Association for Medical Assistance has names of English-speaking doctors and hospitals. Call (716) 754-4883.

Global Assist Hotline (for American Express cardholders) provides emergency medical, legal, and financial assistance. Call (800) 554-2639, or from abroad, call collect (301) 214-8228 to reach multilingual operators twenty-four hours a day. You must have your card number ready.

THE BENEFIT OF TWO-SIGNER TRAVELER'S CHECKS

If one of a couple is sick, the other should be able to pay the bills, so if you rely on traveler's checks, be sure either person can cash them. These are called "two-signer" checks. Or have enough checks in individual names to cover emergency situations.

I spent three weeks in the hospital with pneumonia and didn't know the language well, but the nurses were attentive and one spoke a bit of English. When I returned to the States my own doctor said that the care provided was appropriate and good. But even in France, the hospital food was still hospital food!
—Pam, 52, LeMans, France

RESEARCH YOUR DESTINATION FOR HEALTH AND SAFETY

If you're traveling to a first-world country, you won't need to worry about cholera outbreaks. However, if you intend to travel widely or visit a third-world country, prepare yourself more carefully to avoid health problems. Do basic research about your destination to see if you need special vaccinations or if any health or safety warnings have been issued. Since conditions change, get up-to-date information. Here are a few ways to get it.

SIMPLE PRECAUTIONS

- Ensure that inoculations are current.
- Take immunization records with you.
- Carry any special prescriptions with generic names.
- Take copies of special papers, EKGs, X rays, or dental records as needed.
- Wear a medical ID bracelet if you have a serious health problem.
- Collect the names of doctors, dentists, and good hospitals before you leave.
- Take extra glasses or contacts and the prescription.
- Take insurance cards, forms, and contact numbers.
- As soon as you arrive, learn the local emergency phone numbers for police, fire, and ambulance.
- Locate a physician and a dentist and know where to find emergency facilities.

The Centers for Disease Control and Prevention (CDC)
The CDC in Atlanta, Georgia, has an automated fax system that provides health information twenty-four hours a day. Their *International Travel Directory* documents provide the latest information by topic and provide disease and prevention information for areas throughout the world. Information ranges from vaccine recommendations to special disease outbreak bulletins and additional information such as drugs for malaria or yellow fever.

Request a faxed directory listing the documents available by calling (888) 232-3299. To receive a document, follow the prompts for international health and disease risk information by fax.

The State Department
The State Department provides consular service information at (202) 647-3000. Dial on a phone connected to your fax and follow the recorded instructions. You can order a user guide that explains the types of documents available, then order whatever you need. Documents include consular background information on areas around the world and any special warnings that may have been issued during the past week about possible trouble spots for your health and safety.

DEATH AT A DISTANCE

No one wants to consider death, but it happens to us all once, whether in the United States or overseas. You won't want to lose sleep over the possibility in Portugal or England any more than you would in the States; however, if you become a resident of a foreign country, investigate any special requirements for wills or inheritance taxes should you die outside the United States. Ensure that your family and your own final wishes are taken care of properly.

The U.S. Department of State estimates that about 6,000 Americans die abroad each year, either expats or visitors. The consulate office contacts the next of kin and can help make arrangement for the body to either be buried overseas or returned to the States. If you want to be buried in the family plot in Cincinnati, your body will have to travel back. Some insurance policies cover this, but if not, it will be paid from the remaining estate. The U.S. government will *not* pay for this service.

Wills

Inheritance laws in other countries may surprise you. In some, if you're considered to be domiciled in another country, you will pay their taxes, and your will may be overridden based on the country's requirements. France, for example, has a system whereby children inherit over the surviving spouse. Right. You could find the money you and your spouse saved over the years going to the kid's new Mercedes. Even if they give you a ride with the top down, that's not a surprise you'll want to discover at the last minute.

Don't assume that common sense or your U.S. will takes precedence. It may not in a foreign country, but you can take steps to avoid potential problems and enjoy your adventure with an easy mind.

First of all, if you're merely traveling through a country, staying for just a few weeks or sometimes months, and retain obvious ties to the States, you're a tourist not a resident. In this case, don't worry. If, however, you decide to live overseas for an extended period of time, contact an attorney who specializes in international law to ensure your final wishes will be followed.

HEALTHY TRAVEL CHECKLIST

Prior to Leaving
Medical Check-Up
    Vaccinations as necessary
    Prescriptions
Dental Care
    Cleaning
    Dental work as necessary
Eye Exam
    Update prescription

Take with You
    Prescription medicines
    Prescriptions (using generic names to show physicians overseas)
    Insurance claim forms and contact numbers
    Contact numbers for your previous physician, dentist, or other specialists
    Extra eyeglasses/contacts
    Names of doctors/hospitals overseas
    Xrays, EKGs, or other reports needed for baseline analysis

The Well-Stocked Portable Medicine Chest Includes
    Your prescriptions
    Antibacterial ointment
    Antiseptic soap
    Adhesive tape/bandages
    Antidiarrheal, such as Imodium A-D
    Aspirin or aspirin-free pain reliever
    Cold medication
    Cotton swabs
    Insect repellent
    Sunscreen
    Thermometer

DO'S AND DON'TS FOR FOOD AND DRINK

Some areas of the world require extra vigilance in maintaining your health. Others won't require any more attention than in the States. The following are general recommendations. Investigate your specific destination for requirements.

• Drink bottled water when you travel, unless you know the water is safe and you've become accustomed to it. Even in the U.S. different mineral concentrations could upset a tender stomach, so better safe than sorry.
• In some underdeveloped countries such as Mexico, do not drink tap water, use ice cubes made from it, or brush your teeth with it. Use bottled water.
• Only eat fruits that you've peeled yourself.
• In problem areas, do not eat uncooked vegetables or salads.
• Eat only meats, fish, or shellfish that have been cooked—never raw or undercooked.
• Take a supply of iodine tablets for use where good water is scarce.

20

Protecting Your Person and Property

Murder and mayhem, in general, are not nearly as prevalent overseas as some imaginations make them. I've heard people cite fear as keeping them from traveling overseas—fear of the unknown language and customs, fear of being on a train left by mistake in the depths of a Siberian winter (never mind that they intend to go to the Caribbean), or simply fear of doing something *different*, something far away from the life they've lived for decades.

Some of this is entirely normal and to be expected. It's not, however, a reason to frighten yourself out of having a fabulous experience overseas. Sure, be sensible, but the facts are that, with a little bit of preparation, overseas isn't any more daunting or dangerous than a trip within the States.

Come to think of it, it's probably *less* so. Note the statistics and you'll realize that you've survived one of the most dangerous places in the world—the United States. The United States consistently leads the world in deaths by guns. In many of the areas most midlifers select for their adventure, random acts of violence are much less common. In Britain, guns are outlawed completely. In most Western European countries, rifles are common for hunting but handguns are not.

Your major concern in civilized nations overseas will be petty crimes. You might fear for your passport or wallet, but not your life. (This is assuming you're not planning on running away to retire in a drug lord's stronghold.)

Just as in the United States, small towns tend to be safer than large cities or tourist spots. Hordes of tourists attract pickpockets like candy does a child. If you're heading for a major city or other tourist attraction, be aware and a tad more careful. As when traveling in the United States, common sense usually wins out.

PERSONAL SAFETY

Is It a Trouble Spot or Not?

I assume you're looking for a pleasurable experience and plan to avoid war zones or areas in the path of an active volcano. To find out more on the safety of various areas you plan to visit, the U.S. State Department provides Consular Information Sheets with information on crime, health risks, security concerns, areas of unrest, type of government, important laws, location of embassies, currency information, and much more on every country in the world.

Specific travel warnings are issued when the State Department decides that Americans should avoid traveling to a country completely. For a list of current consular information sheets and travel warnings, call the Overseas Citizens Services Department at (202) 647-5225 from a Touch-Tone phone. You'll hear a recording with current information. The information is also available at the regional passport agencies, field offices of the U.S. Department of Commerce, and U.S. embassies and consulates abroad.

For consular information via your fax machine, dial (202) 647-3000 and pick up the handset to use it as if it's a regular telephone; the system will tell you how to order the various publications.

To access U.S. consular travel information via the Internet, log on to travel.state.gov. This Web page also provides access to other international information, including travel publications, passport information, international legal assistance, health information, and much more.

> *In Guadalajara, one can hear a concert of some sort almost*
> *every evening. As you stroll the plazas, perfectly safely in the evenings,*
> *you're serenaded with soft strains from marimbas. No matter the economic*
> *status of the Mexican citizen, they are a smiling people.*
> —Bess, 77, Mexico

Handy Tips for Travelers

The Department of State puts out a series of brochures called *Tips for Travelers,* which cover specific regions of the world, ranging from South Asia, the Middle East and North Africa, Russia, the Caribbean, Mexico, and Canada.

The brochures cover a country's currency, customs regulations, import and export controls, and other such practicalities. Order by calling (202) 512-1800. The cost is $1 to $1.50 each.

Keeping Up with the Laws

Know the laws in the country you'll be visiting. Drug laws are frequently much harsher. Even prescription drugs, such as tranquilizers, may create a problem in some countries. If in doubt, ask local authorities or your embassy or consulate.

In Mexico, firearms can get you up to thirty years in prison—just for having one in your possession. Photography can get you in trouble in some countries if you shoot military installations, government buildings, or border areas. If in doubt, ask.

You can get information on your destination's laws from a travel agent, tourist bureaus, embassies, and consulates.

Personal safety was a great consideration to our living here. All Swiss males must serve in the military, so they all have a fully automatic assault rifle with ammunition at home, yet there are no mass murders or random shootings.
—Edward, 37, Geneva, Switzerland

Tips to Ensure Your Personal Safety

Common sense protects you in most situations. Here are a few of the rules to keep in mind:
• Know the main trouble spots before you go and avoid them.
• Be aware at automatic teller machines.
• Know the area and use common sense. There's a big difference in walking back from dinner at midnight along the popular Left Bank in Paris and wandering a dark alley in Amsterdam's red light district at 4 A.M.

Should You Be Concerned about Terrorism?

Unless you're a war correspondent or politician, in most cases and in most places the average person visits, you will not be a target of terrorists. Frankly, they have better things to do than target a casual tourist that they didn't even know was going to be visiting the Taj Mahal that day.

Here are a few general rules to keep in mind:
• Note suspicious abandoned packages or briefcases in public areas, such as airports or train stations. Report them to security officials and leave the area.
• Be aware of current problems with terrorism. To find out areas under threat, see the consular travel information and travel warnings mentioned previously.
• Avoid locales that are obvious terrorist targets.
• Try to minimize time in public transportation areas.

Protecting Your Belongings

The major concern in many locales is to protect yourself from petty crime. As John remarks, "I'm not worried about myself overseas, just my wallet!" Mainly, you're concerned about your passport, credit cards, cash, and travel documents.

Pickpocket Tricks and How to Avoid Them

In some countries, violence against people is considerably less prevalent than in the United States, but pickpockets are the scourge. They'll target the unwary traveler—or the resident who should know better. My friend Gail has lived in Paris for seventeen years. She's a friendly, easygoing person who, unfortunately, has been the victim of purse snatchers three times there. Learn from her mistakes. One time she put her purse into her baby's stroller, turned to look at a shirt in the store, and turned back to find the purse gone. Another time she was in the Metro when a teen stopped the turnstile. While she was distracted by him, his partner grabbed her purse and ran.

There are variations to the turnstile episode above. They all work on the principle of distraction. One person jostles you or points to something in the sky or trips you, while their partner grabs your wallet or purse. The best solution is to be aware of people near you and keep valuables out of sight.

If a bunch of kids surrounds you asking for money, back off and tell them loudly to leave you alone. Attracting attention is the last thing they want to do, so don't be shy about protecting your space.

Protecting Yourself While Traveling

- Use covered luggage tags to make your identity or nationality less obvious. Put your name, address, and phone number on a paper inside the bag as well. Then lock your luggage.
- Never leave luggage unattended in airports. If not stolen, it could worry someone and become fodder for the bomb squad.
- If traveling overnight on a train, lock your compartment or, if you have a traveling companion, take turns sleeping.
- Be aware of unusual activity near the door of the compartment. Robbers have been know to use sleeping gas in train compartments.
- Don't accept food or drink from strangers; it could be drugged.

Smart Ways to Keep Your Belongings Safe

- Dress conservatively. Don't flaunt jewelry or expensive belongings.
- Put your main money stash, credit cards, and passport where no one could possibly grab them. Use a hidden travel pocket under your clothes.
- If you use a waist pack, make sure it has a strong clasp. I have one with a zipper pocket that is at the back of the fanny pack, against my body. No

one can pick it, though they could cut the waist strap. Some specialty stores and travel catalogs carry waist packs with a metal cord through the belt portion, so it can't be cut. I've never gone this far, but it's an idea if you're an absent-minded professor and might not be aware of someone that close to you.

• Keep pocket change where you can reach it easily. Not so much you'd miss it if it was stolen, but enough so you can handle a postcard or cup of coffee on the street without advertising where your real stash is. Replenish this inconspicuously as you spend down the pocket change.

• If you use a shoulder bag, wear it with the strap crossed over your body, never just hanging from your shoulder. Most women in Europe do this, often keeping their hand on the bag, almost automatically as they walk down busy pedestrian streets.

• Walk with your bag away from the curb to avoid purse snatchers on motorcycles.

• Be aware at automatic teller machines.

• Don't use the ATM in a lonely spot at night.

• Don't count your cash in public.

• If the worst happens and you're confronted, don't fight. Your money and passport can be replaced. You can't.

Paper Precautions

Your identity is something that's important overseas. You might have to replace your passport or prove you are who you say you are to cash a check.

• Before you leave the States, make copies of important papers to expedite their replacement if necessary. Make photocopies of the first pages of your passport and your driver's license. Bring an extra set of passport photos too.

• Make photocopies of your air tickets, credit cards, and driver's license. Carry one copy separately; leave one with family or friends at home.

• If you have traveler's checks, make a note of the serial numbers and carry the note separately. Cross the numbers off as you use the checks.

• If you've got a bad memory, jot down the number you need for your cash machine card or other vital numbers, but add a code to the number. For example, if your withdrawal card code is 4567 add two to each number and jot down 6789. Or add your birthday date to the real number, for example 4/2/40 would make the number 8707.

• Bring a copy of your birth certificate and marriage certificate overseas to arrange legal details, such as a house purchase. Leave the originals at home with family members or in a safe deposit box. Remember, though, that anything in the safe deposit box will be unreachable unless you fly home to get it. You may choose to give power of attorney to a trusted family member or friend to get into the box.

I'm not worried about drive-by shootings here.
Maybe a drive-by splashing by a tractor on the wine route . . .
—John, 62, Loire Valley, France

On the Road

- Choose a common car for the local area, and if it's a rental, request that markings that show it to be a rental be removed.
- Keep doors locked at all times.
- Wear seat belts, of course. It's usually the law overseas, as well as in the States.
- When driving in a strange area, know where you're heading before you set off, especially at night. If in doubt, don't drive at night.
- If you must park and leave belongings in the car, keep everything in the trunk, so your car interior is as bare as Yul Brenner's head.
- Do *not* open the car trunk at tourist sites unless you're removing everything in it. One couple arrived in Rome and decided to see the Coliseum prior to checking into their hotel. They drove into the parking lot where they carefully and obviously tucked all their luggage into the trunk, locked it, and went sightseeing. Well, of course, it was gone when they returned.
- If you must put things in the trunk, stop and do so *before* you reach your destination. When you arrive, simply lock the car and leave as though you had nothing more important than a litter bag.

Hotels

- Be aware at the registration desk if a large group arrives with you.
- Don't just drop your luggage on the floor and walk away; you could lose it.
- Keep hotel doors locked.
- Meet visitors you don't know in the lobby.
- Don't give out the number to your hotel room; this includes not flashing the key about when you leave the hotel or asking loudly for your room key.
- Don't leave valuables in the room when you're out; use the hotel safe.

What U.S. Consulates Do and Don't

They do . . .
Issue visas to foreigners
Help U.S. citizens abroad
- Replace a passport
- Help find medical assistance
- Help get funds from family, bank, or employer
- Help in an emergency, to relay an urgent message, for example
- Visit Americans arrested and in jail
- Make arrangements after death
- Help in disaster/evacuation
- Issue reports of births
- Issue passports
- Distribute federal benefits payments
- Assist in child custody disputes
- Help handle personal estates of deceased U.S. citizens
- Assist with absentee voting
- Notarize documents
- Advise on property claims
- Provide U.S. tax forms
- Assist U.S. courts in legal matters

They don't . . .
- Provide travel advice
- Act as a bank, lawyer, or law enforcement officer
- Find employment or a place to live
- Act as interpreters
- Search for missing luggage
- Settle disputes with local people

However, they can tell you how to get help on these matters.

Problems and How to Handle Them

If you have serious medical, legal, or financial problems overseas, contact the nearest U.S. Embassy or consulate. Though the personnel there cannot serve as doctors, lawyers, or bankers, they keep lists of such people and advise U.S. citizens on a variety of topics. Embassy or consulate personnel can help you get in touch with family or friends in the States for other assistance, whether money or moral support.

A Lost Passport

Your U.S. passport can usually be replaced at the nearest U.S. consulate. This is why extra photos come in handy. With these and a driver's license, credit cards, or other identification proving who you are, you can replace your passport more easily.

Robbery

Report a robbery immediately to the local police. Their written report will establish your claim for your insurance company. Sometimes, your homeowner policy will cover the loss of luggage, but check that it's still valid before you leave for overseas. If you have sold or rented your home, the policy that used to cover you may no longer be in effect.

If your credit cards are stolen, contact the bank or credit card issuers immediately. Keep the phone numbers separate from the cards and in a place where they can be easily located in an emergency.

Emergency Funds

The Department of State's Overseas Citizen's Services can come in handy for Americans in emergency situations. Contact the nearest U.S. embassy. If your emergency is financial, the consular office can allow you to call home collect to arrange to get funds. Your bank or relatives can wire money using the U.S. embassy as your conduit for a faster response. If they wire the money through the State Department in Washington, D.C., as soon as the money is received there, the embassy or consulate near you will be authorized to turn over the equivalent amount to you overseas.

For more information about the Bureau of Consular Affairs, their home page on the Internet is travel.state.gov.

Homeowner Policies for Overseas Coverage

I never thought it necessary to have special insurance on my belongings other than the homeowners policy on our home overseas and, of course, insurance on our car. However, there are companies that insure belongings specifically for travelers. Often this insurance comes complete with personal accident or trip cancellation policies.

Some companies that offer comprehensive policies include

Access America, Inc., P.O. Box 90315, Richmond, VA 23286-4991; telephone (800) 284-8300. Travel insurance and trip cancellation, medical insurance for the short term trips, and baggage and travel accident insurance.

Travel Guard International, 1145 Clark Street, Stevens Point, WI 54481; telephone (800) 782-5151 or (715) 345-0505. Offers baggage, trip cancellation, and medical insurance for the length of a short trip.

Now Go Forth and Don't Worry

It may seem from all the previous tips that the world outside the United States is a very frightening place. In reality, the only danger you might face would be a waitress who spills your cappuccino. Like many Americans overseas, chances are you'll feel safer many places there than in the States. Safety is high on the list for many people in explaining why they enjoy living overseas.

21

Your Countdown Checklist

IF I SHOULD NOT BE LEARNING
NOW, WHEN SHOULD I BE?
—Lacydes

The secret to a successful adventure hinges on three things: planning, planning, and planning. You can't manage a long-term change in lifestyle without a map to guide you. The sooner you start creating one, the better you'll stay on track, avoiding pitfalls that can sabotage the experience. If an unforeseen problem does arise, a plan will keep you organized enough to cut that mountain down into a molehill.

So don't trust your memory. Make lists galore of everything you need to do at each stage. Constantly update the lists, crossing off, adding, making sublists of lists as the time draws closer to departure. You'll know you're doing it right if you could end up papering a moving van with the castoffs.

Here's a basic checklist to begin the planning process:

A Year to Six Months in Advance
• Research destinations.
• Network with friends and acquaintances.
• Do major repairs on house in preparation for rental or sale.
• Start allowing unwanted magazine subscriptions to lapse.

Five Months
• Determine what to do with belongings.

- Hold a preliminary garage sale if necessary.
- Put your house on the market (if selling).
- Determine if you need a visa and, if necessary, start the application procedure.

Three Months
- Save address labels for change-of-address forms.
- Put ads in the paper for house rental (if renting).
- Set up a complete address book for travel.

Two Months
- If planning to take a computer, buy it and practice on it.
- Visit doctors for checkups.
- Arrange for prescriptions and extra prescription medicine.
- Visit your eye doctor.
- Get new lenses/glasses, if necessary.
- Arrange for PO box or mail delivery.
- Change address, if necessary, to PO box.
- Determine what to take, sell, and give away.
- Set up a new bank account for overseas.
- Ensure you have checks and an automatic withdrawal card.
- Get shots for your pet (more than thirty days in advance).
- Arrange transportation.

One Month
- Cancel utilities.
- Start packing.
- Buy special items you want to take with you.
- Copy important papers.
- Visit friends and family for good-byes.

One Week
- Store furniture.

Three Days
- Health certificate for animals (check requirements for specific country).

One Day
- Take a deep breath and handle final details.

The Day
- Wave goodbye and head off for the experience of a lifetime, knowing you've prepared well to enjoy every minute to its fullest.

22

Settling In

THE MORE I TRAVELED THE MORE
I REALIZED THAT FEAR MAKES STRANGERS
OF PEOPLE WHO WOULD BE FRIENDS.
—Shirley MacLaine

Finally, the happy day arrives. You can hardly believe that you're about to take off for an adventure overseas, free from daily constraints, prepared to explore old-world cities, relax on a beach, or visit every museum in the exotic locale you've picked for your destination.

So many new impressions pour over you that the days pass in a blur. You try to remember the details to tell the family and friends back home—the child tugging at his mother's full cotton skirts in a local market, the sunset over a Romanesque chapel, the sound of cowbells in that mountain village. Soon you've got so many memories stored up, you'll never remember them all. Make the time to write a diary and jot down your impressions. They'll bring the experiences back into focus for you later, and they form the base for wonderful letters home when you finally have time to write them.

This initial excitement can make you feel like a child again, eager to see every sight, taste every delicious-looking morsel. Remember, you're here for more than a vacation, so there's time. Pace yourself and enjoy the experience. Take the first few days to get settled into your new environment and start feeling comfortable. If you've planned well, you'll already know what to expect in general. However, you'll still be undergoing vast new changes in your way of life. Allow yourself some slack time to rest and take it all in.

As much as you planned before your adventure, do the reverse now. Don't overplan and jam too much into each day. I guarantee you that every-thing will take longer than you think, at first, because you're feeling your way in a new culture. This is doubly true if you're trying out a new language.

Just shopping for new socks, which might take you half an hour at a department store in the States, can take a day when you're living your adventure—not necessarily due to inefficiencies in shopping, but there's so much to do along the way. You start out in the morning and see this funky little street with a charming coffee shop. One little cup wouldn't hurt, would it? Then you pass an interesting church and pop inside for "just a minute" to see the stained glass windows. You find a store, but they don't carry socks or the style you want, so you head for another one. By now it's lunchtime and the store you want is closed. After lunch you find the socks but spend forty-five minutes figuring out your size in the metric system. Once you do that, you get to pay with all that colorful "play money."

One reason everything takes longer is that you're having so much fun being sidetracked doing it.

> *I first moved to England and we thought the language was*
> *the same but it isn't! One time this lovely lady came to tea and talked*
> *about "humping the vicar after church." Turns out it meant giving him*
> *a lift. It made us think we should start writing a dictionary.*
> —Judy, 62, Athens, Greece

IMMEDIATE CHORES

Fun is fun, but unlike a vacation, moving overseas for any length of time will involve you in some chores to get settled. One of the first ones is to register with the local authorities for your long-stay visa, if you need one, and/or with the American embassy.

If you have a regular mailing address, go to the local post office and introduce yourself. In some locations overseas, the addresses can be rather ambiguous, using just a house name, not a street address. If so, let the local post office know that any mail addressed to Mr. and Mrs. America at the "House of the Two Lizards" belongs to you.

If you don't already have names of recommended doctors, dentists, and hospitals, ask other expats or locals you meet. One good name leads to another. If you find a good doctor, he or she can often recommend special-ists. If you are in need of a specialist due to an existing condition, visit them before it's an emergency. They'll be familiar with you and you'll be more comfortable knowing who to call if the need arises.

The Next Several Weeks

Explore your new town and uncover the lowest price gasoline, the freshest food market, the handiest hardware store. Meet the local people, smile nicely, and get to know them. In many countries, services are provided on a more personalized basis than Americans may be used to. This goes for the baker, the butcher, the electrician, and other services.

The system can work for you or against you. When we first moved, the power went out in our rental house on the Friday night of a long holiday weekend, I couldn't get an electrician to respond. Even my tempting question about overtime pay didn't elicit much interest. "But it's the holiday." Now that we're more settled, we've located "our electrician," and we've used him for numerous small jobs around the house, so he's available at a moment's notice.

This process is ongoing. As you live overseas longer, you'll meet new friends who are more than willing to share their insights and recommendations.

> *Because our interests and goals were the same it*
> *mattered not the country of origin. We made friendships with*
> *numerous other couples traveling along our path, friendships which*
> *continued as we returned to our respective countries.*
> —Sue and Jim, worldwide cruisers

Tripping over English Speakers

Unless you've lived overseas before, you may be surprised how many Americans, Brits, and Australians have come before you. These form a ready-made group of English speakers just waiting for other English speakers to show up. They'll ply you with information on everything from where to find the most mouthwatering pastries to the best real estate agent, plumber, and English-language bookstore. You'll share tales of your voyages and find new places to try based on others' recommendations.

The fact that there are so many English speakers looking for kindred souls makes your adventure easier. It also makes it more difficult because it's tempting to slip into a routine of socializing only with English speakers, a crutch that eventually becomes a barrier to meeting people of other nationalities. This is especially true if you limit yourself to other Americans, in which case sooner or later you'll begin to feel like you haven't lived an adventure, but instead are living in an American camp.

*I think the key to living in a foreign country is to get acquainted
with the local people and try not to latch on to your countrymen. That's
where we made our mistake in the beginning. I think the Venezuelan
friends we have made would do anything for us in a time of need.*
—Susan, 65, Caracas, Venezuela

*I speak a little Italian, but not much. My boyfriend's Italian and
doesn't speak English. It works out wonderfully because we can't fight!*
—Barbara, 47, Florence, Italy

MEETING THE NATIVES

Becoming involved with local people adds to the charm of your stay over-seas. Sometimes it's a bit tougher than making English-speaking friends but it can be done. The trick is to know enough of the language to start speaking with someone.

You don't have to be proficient by any means. Often people overseas would like the opportunity to practice the English they learned in school. If you're living in a small town, you can't remain anonymous in any case. People will tell others about the "Americans" living down the street.

This resulted in one of our best friendships. One Sunday about six weeks after we had moved into our rented house, a couple and their two young sons knocked at the door. Rosa was going to visit her American father—whom she hadn't seen in thirty-four years. He'd forgotten his French. She didn't speak English. Would we make a phone call to ensure that the plans were correct for the rendezvous at the airport? Of course we did, sharing a bottle of wine at their house. The next time they needed a phone call, they insisted on fixing a five-course French meal. We are now involved in their lives, and they've been a wonderful help to us as well, providing tidbits of advice. But don't wait for people to knock on the door. Here are some ways you can hurry the integration into your new environment.

*Learning the language is important, not just for communication,
but for basic cultural understanding. It still takes most people at least
three to five years to feel really at home in a foreign language.*
—Doug, 43, Basel, Switzerland

Take a Local Class

Some groups overseas are created and run for English speakers, so of course, you'll meet lots of expats this way. To become involved with local people and practice your language skills, sign up for a community group. A little investigation will uncover art classes, music groups, cooking, tennis, swimming, hiking, biking. You name it.

John, who knew very little French, happened to pass by a small storefront art class and discovered an informal group that meets every Saturday. He signed up. Though he doesn't understand all the teacher's instructions, the group is convivial, and now he's invited to social events and art shows with the students, the teacher, and their families.

It even led to his being invited to paint on Saturdays in the town square with other artists, which in turn led to meeting more friends of friends. And so the circle grows.

All our friends have been "locals." They are nice and
tolerate our weak French, but I need a woman I can chat with!
—Chris, 50, Paris, France

Participate in a Sport
People overseas like to walk, hike, play tennis, ski, ride bikes, and take part in other sports you may enjoy. Ask at the local tourist bureau for information. Look for posters advertising group activities. Sometimes notes are posted on local church or grocery bulletin boards. If you see a sign posted for nature walks on Sunday morning, sign up. You'll get exercise and meet people at the same time.

Talk to Merchants
Patronize shops in the neighborhood and become known to proprietors and clerks. They'll remember you, and you'll feel more at home returning to Carlo's butcher shop or Michelle's bakery. The ambience is much more fun than in a supermarket chain and eventually, as you become part of the community, you'll get a better cut of meat or perfectly browned bread!

Attend Church
If you belong to a specific denomination, introduce yourself to the minister, priest, or rabbi. As in the United States, these religious affiliations lead to social events that are put on by church members and in which you can participate to meet new friends.

Volunteer
Just as in the States, people in communities overseas need volunteers to help with community projects. Sign up in your community to help run the local fair, help beautify the town square, or teach kids English.

Gail, a long-time American expat, is a full-time English teacher who encourages volunteers among the English-speaking community to speak to her young foreign students. She has the English speakers talk about a hobby or interest to help the students hear the real thing from someone new.

Communities overseas are like anywhere else. If you participate, you become acclimated and make new friends. If you don't, you'll be on the periphery of life. Get involved and deepen the pleasure of the adventure.

Handling Hordes of Visitors

Everyone who moves overseas invites everyone back home to visit. Then sooner or later, everyone who moves overseas begins to wonder why they were so loose with the invitations. You may be a perfectly sociable sort and we all like visitors, but there comes a time when the washing machine can't keep up with the changing of the towels, and the budget just won't cover another week of touring with indefatigable friends or relatives.

Be prepared with a few ground rules. These are perfectly acceptable among civilized hosts and guests, and ensure that both enjoy the visit more thoroughly:

Guests Must Have Transportation. Squiring people around in your vehicle for two weeks is exhausting and frustrating for both parties. You may want to put your feet up or even do your wash. They want to pack every sight they can into their two weeks' vacation. This is especially onerous when you have back-to-back guests. The second group gets the watered-down tour, and you end up feeling guilty that you didn't do more. With their own rental car or plans to use buses or trains, you'll all be happier.

Guests Take Responsibility for Their Own Plans. Be wary of the visitor who says, "Oh, you know the area, just take me where you think best." You may have different interests and in any case, you're then responsible for showing them the sites. See the transportation comment above! If they need advice, of course give it. This helps if you have plenty of information available for them to read, with some maps helping them find their way around.

Collect a File of Local Sites. Visit tourist offices in your area and collect brochures on the different tourist sites within a day's drive. Hand these to your guests and let them pick their own day trips. If they don't, then assume they want to sit in your backyard and smell the flowers.

Don't Be Shy about Asking Guests to Contribute. I hope your guests are polite enough to offer to buy groceries while there or treat you to a dinner out as their contribution to having a free room for their vacation. They also should clean up after themselves and help prepare meals with you. If they, however, seem remiss in this matter, just say cheerfully, "Hey, I was wondering if you'd help make dinner tonight." Or, "We usually ask guests to prepare a meal one day a week while they're staying with us. I hope you won't mind." They'd have to be boors to say no. If they do, you know never to invite them again.

Once you are situated in Europe, people you once considered acquaintances will now consider you bosom buddies.
—Claire, 45, Algarve, Portugal

Overcoming Culture Shock

You may do all the right things to find new friends, share your home with old ones, discover new interests, and still suddenly find yourself running head-on into culture shock. It can be brought on by the simplest things: The shopkeeper in Italy doesn't stock your brand of toothpaste; you can't find the new mystery (in English) anywhere; the electricity in your rental house cops out when you run the washer and the vacuum at the same time.

Once the initial excitement is over—heck, maybe even the minute you set foot on foreign soil— you'll begin comparing the new location with the States. Try to remember, however, that if you wanted the same experience, you could have stayed in the comfort of your same-old-same-old living room.

Have patience. Regard the merely unpleasant with a sense of adventure and consider it as an interesting story to tell family and friends back home later, when the distance provides some humor.

One final note: If you are seriously unhappy overseas, you can always go home again. But make sure that your misery is not just a temporary situation brought on by exhaustion or two weeks of unseasonable rain and cold weather. You could have been this unhappy at "home" too. Give yourself some time, and often you'll discover that you adapt and enjoy the very aspects of a culture that at first may have shocked or dismayed you.

You've got to take charge. To avoid that letdown feeling of being alone overseas during the holidays, we started having a Christmas afternoon open house. So we're busy planning and having friends stop over.
Anne, 61, Albufeira, Portugal

23

Return of the Native

IT IS HARD TO FAIL, BUT IT
IS WORSE NEVER TO HAVE TRIED.
—Theodore Roosevelt

Your adventure overseas will end when you return to the States, but this is not the end of the story. The memories of your trip will linger, providing pleasure long after the adventure ends. The friends you've encountered will be spread far and wide, and like Johnny Appleseed's trees, they'll flavor the following years through correspondence and future visits. The new foods you've learned to appreciate will spice your meals with variety and conversation as you share them with family and friends. Certainly, you've gathered enough tales of adventure to hold court at cocktail parties for ten years to come.

Still, when all is said and done, you will return to pick up your life where you left it . . . or will you? You may physically return to the exact same city, the exact same neighborhood, the exact same house, but, like the child who grows and returns to his old room after years away, the room that seemed so large seems to have shrunk.

You'll discover differences, of course, in your neighborhood and in your friends and family. A new mall took over the old dry cleaning plant or cousin Holly grew a beard. None of these superficial changes will come close to the changes that occurred within yourself. You've expanded your horizons and your mind by encountering the world outside the United States. You've come back a changed person, while many of your neighbors may have simply changed television channels.

They may be excited to tell you about all the changes in the neighborhood since you left. They may also like to hear your travel tales. But what many returning expats have discovered is that the original base of commonality has been eroded.

After tasting gelato in Rome, you may be less than interested in the fact that there's a new ice cream store around the block. The other situation that arises is that, once the initial excitement of your return is over, any mention of an adventure overseas will make it appear as though you're bragging, only you're dropping names like Paris and Barcelona instead of movie stars. Even if your friends never tire of your stories, many of the adventures you're so fond of will be beyond their comprehension.

> *The worst part of living overseas? Coming back! We had time*
> *to travel. Now we're back but it was a strange sensation, almost as though*
> *we were strangers here. Once you've gained a global perspective it's tough*
> *to relate to people who've lived their whole lives in suburbia.*
> —Susan, 45, formerly Bahrain

In addition, due to the fluke of geography that isolates the United States, many people in the United States are able to isolate themselves from world events. The United States is a big country, and the news tends to concentrate within the country's borders. This lack of knowledge may seem narrow-minded once you've become acclimated to international living, with the world perspective that accompanies it.

I tell you the above not to discourage you, but to prepare you. Many people I spoke to called returning to the States more difficult than encountering the new culture overseas. Forewarned is forearmed, and hopefully, if you keep this in mind, you won't feel quite as let down when you discover that reintegrating into your old life is not as easy as you may have expected.

> *I get culture shock when I go back to the States to visit. Then*
> *people say it's inefficient here [in Greece] and they can't imagine why*
> *I stay. But I wouldn't know where to go in the States and I love Greece.*
> *One minute it's twentieth century, the next it's the tenth!*
> —Judy, 62, Athens, Greece

You can readapt, but hopefully with new interests and resources, just as you adapted to your adventure and new country overseas. By not expecting to fit immediately back into the same square peg, you may round out your life in new ways in the States.

One way is to seek out others who have the new mind-set you've discovered. Join or start a French or Spanish or whatever-language-you-learned club. Volunteer at a local elementary school to talk about your adventures and tell the kids about life overseas. Become part of the international community in your city or town. Maintain contact with your friends overseas and invite them to visit you. In this way, you can extend the pleasure of your time abroad for many years after you return.

The big question many people ask those of us who have chosen a long-term adventure overseas is: When will you return? Six months? A year? Five or more?

Some people can answer immediately. They know their sabbatical is for a set amount of time, the length of a professional assignment of two years, for example. Others simply say, "As long as I'm enjoying myself."

Once they're settled overseas, some people discover that the lifestyle suits them, and they extend the stay—again and again. Finally, some know that they won't return at all. As Claire in Portugal says, "The family will just visit us here. We can't see any reason to go back."

Of course, many grown-ups running away for the adventure will eventually miss family and friends and want the comfort of familiar U.S. soil. Often, even long-time expats return when they are older to be near children or settle down from the rigors of travel. But expats must be a hearty bunch because I noted that many considered returning only after they were eighty or older.

The time frame you choose will be subject to your own lifestyle, family, age, and desires. Whenever you choose to return from your overseas adventure, you will be enriched by the experience for your remaining days.

Coming back after extensive time overseas is far more difficult than the going because life there tends to be far more fulfilling and broadening.
— Getra, 51, formerly Switzerland and Africa

Bibliography

A TRAVELER WITHOUT KNOWLEDGE
IS A BIRD WITHOUT WINGS.
—Sadi Gulistan

No bibliography could compete with the wealth of information available in the travel section of your local bookstore or library. There you'll find stacks of books that will help you investigate specific destinations. A little more digging will provide detailed information on cultures and customs overseas, international job or study opportunities, and a myriad of tales written by others who've lived or traveled frequently overseas.

Obviously, the bibliography below is by no means a complete list. It is, however, a compilation of some of the books I found to be particularly interesting and useful in researching an adventure abroad.

DESTINATION REFERENCE

The World's Top Retirement Havens by Carol and Dan Thalimer (Santa Fe, NM: John Muir Publications, 1998). A directory of potential areas for retirement overseas. Discusses vital aspects involved in selecting a locale, including weather, taxes, cost of living, and available health care.

Living and Working in France; Living and Working in Spain; Living and Working in Britain; Living and Working in Switzerland by David Hampshire (Haddam, CT: Survival Books). Practical and easy-to-read books provide essential information on the details of setting up a household overseas, from choosing lodgings to health care to dialing the phone!

Choose Mexico: Retire on $600 a Month by John Howells and Don Merwin (Oakland, CA: Gateway Books, 1994). Inspirational for anyone who thinks they can't afford to retire and have an interesting lifestyle.

Your Guide to Retiring to Mexico, Costa Rica and Beyond by Shelley Emling (Garden City Park, NY: Avery Publishing Group). Information and resources for living in Mexico, Costa Rica, Guatemala, and Ecuador.

Choose Spain by John Howells and Bettie Magee (Oakland, CA: Gateway Books, out of print). Despite the title, this book provides lifestyle information for both Spain and neighboring Portugal.

Choose Latin America by John Howells (Oakland, CA: Gateway Books, out of print). Provides information on Central and South America, including cost of living, safety, climate, customs, health care, and more.

International Living, 105 W. Monument St., Baltimore, Maryland 21201; telephone (410) 223-2605; fax (410) 223-2619; e-mail 103114,2472@compuserve.com. Newsletter on life in various countries around the world provides examples of availability and costs for housing, food, and medical care. The annual Quality of Life issue in January ranks the world's best places to live by factors such as stability, health, cultural opportunities, and cost of living.

Adventures in Mexico (AIM). Published by Lloyd Wilkinson, APDO 31-70, Guadalajara, 45050, Jalisco, Mexico. Newsletter on retirement and travel in Mexico by one who's lived there for decades.

Living, Studying, and Working in Italy by Travis Neighbor and Monica Larner (New York: Henry Holt & Co., 1996). Full of helpful insights for those considering Italy as a destination. Did you know, for instance, that Italian law forbids landlords from evicting citizens from residences, so Americans often enjoy an advantage in securing a home?

Transitions Abroad: The Guide to Learning, Living, and Working Overseas, 18 Hulst Road, PO Box 1300, Amherst, MA 01004-1300. Bimonthly magazine for active travelers. Much of it is more applicable to younger travelers, but adult adventurers will find helpful resources as well.

Traveler's Guide to European Camping by Mike and Terri Church (Kirkland, WA: Rolling Homes Press, 1996). Campground descriptions, plus hints on good side trips close to the site, camping strategies, and information on renting an RV or tenting economically in Europe.

1997 Eurail Guide to World Train Travel (Boston: Houghton Mifflin Company, 1997). Covers timetables, service details, and prices for Eurail, Britrail, and other pass options in over a hundred countries, including base cities and over 2000 intermediate stops. Note: Use this as a general guide for cities and stops, but be sure to look for updated information on specific times and prices since they are subject to change.

Eurail 97 Guide to Train Travel in the New Europe (Boston: Houghton Mifflin, 1997). Basically same format as *World Train Travel* above, but specifically geared to Europe.

Lifestyle Decisions/Expat Lifestyles

Your Money or Your Life by Joe Dominguez and Vicki Robin (New York: Penguin Books, 1993). Powerful inspiration, along with practical methods for transforming your life by achieving financial independence.

O Come Ye Back to Ireland by Niall Williams and Christine Breen (New York: Soho Press, 1989). American/Irish couple give up a busy New York lifestyle to farm in the west of Ireland.

A Year in Provence by Peter Mayle (New York: Vintage Books, 1990). Is there anyone who hasn't heard of this book? If you're interested in France, not just Provence, you'll be fascinated.

GUIDEBOOKS

Europe Through the Back Door by Rick Steves (Santa Fe, NM: John Muir Publications, 1998, updated yearly). A tour book that is an all-time favorite due to its emphasis on "down-home" travel, which is less expensive and closer to the local people and culture—more like living there.

Frommer's Guides Series (Old Tappan, NJ: MacMillan Travel, updated yearly). General travel guide that provides some hotel and restaurant suggestions.

Karen Brown's Country Inn Guides series (San Mateo, CA: Travel Press). An excellent series of insightful tips on bed and breakfasts and small inns. Individual books cover various European countries, including Italy, Germany, England, Scotland, France, Spain, and Scandinavia.

Michelin Guides series (Michelin Tyre PLC). The company publishes "Green Guides" for tourism information and "Red Guides" for hotels and restaurant suggestions. Well regarded for information in a handy size for travel.

Insight Guides series (Boston: Houghton Mifflin). Beautifully designed, easy-to-read guides that don't provide names of hotels or restaurants but do provide lush photos to give a wonderful feel for the area covered.

CULTURAL GUIDES

Culture Shock! series (Portland, OR: Graphic Arts Center Publishing). Helpful and fascinating input on customs and etiquette. Books cover numerous destinations, including Australia, Borneo, Britain, France, India, Israel, Japan, Norway, Philippines, South Africa, Spain, Thailand, and many more!

Do's and Taboos Around the World, edited by Roger E. Axtell (New York: John Wiley and Sons, 1993). Is it all right to make the "OK" sign? Should you cross your legs or keep your feet on the floor? This book will tell you. Fun and interesting.

Kiss, Bow, or Shake Hands: How to Do Business in Sixty Countries by Terri Morrison, Wayne A. Conaway, and George A. Borden, Ph.D. (Holbrook, MA: Adams Media Corp., 1994). Designed for businesspeople, but the information is also handy for anyone wanting to understand cultural differences.

Survival Kit for Overseas Living by L. Robert Kohls (Yarmouth, ME: Intercultural Press, 1996). Recommended book for anyone wanting to increase their chances of success in the live-abroad experience.

Learning

The ISS Directory of Overseas Schools by International Schools Services (Princeton, NJ: International Schools Services, updated yearly). Comprehensive guide to American and international schools worldwide, including K–12 schools, boarding schools, and international baccalaureate schools.

Peterson's Learning Adventures Around the World, edited by Peter S. Greenberg (Princeton, NJ: Peterson's, updated yearly). Extensive reference to cultural and archaeological tours, academic and language courses, volunteer programs, and spiritual centers.

Smart Vacations (The Traveler's Guide to Learning Adventures Abroad), Council on International Educational Exchange, edited by Priscilla Tovey (New York: St. Martin's Press, 1993). Ideas for expanding your mind while exploring the world.

International Directory of Voluntary Work by Victoria Pybus (Princeton, NJ: Peterson's, 1993). Lists and information on volunteer opportunities overseas.

Computer Reference

Net Travel: How Travelers Use the Internet by Michael Shapiro (Cambridge, MA: O'Reilly & Associates, 1997). Everything you ever wanted to know and more to find travel information via the Internet.

Index